To Owen
From Joan
1975

"I desire a mysterious art, always reminding
and half reminding those who understand it of dearly
loved things, doing its work by suggestion, not by
direct statement, a complexity of rhythm, color,
gesture, not space pervading like the intellect but
a memory and a prophecy."

Yeats

The Symphonies of
Ralph Vaughan Williams

THE SYMPHONIES OF

RALPH VAUGHAN WILLIAMS

ELLIOTT S. SCHWARTZ

THE UNIVERSITY OF MASSACHUSETTS PRESS

AMHERST, 1964

Library of Congress Catalog Card Number: 64-24402

Printed in the United States of America

Howard Kirshen, Printing
Boston, Massachusetts

To My Parents

Nathan and Rose Schwartz

Preface

WHEN RALPH VAUGHAN WILLIAMS DIED on August 26, 1958 at the age of 86, the musical world lost one of the few creative giants of the first half of this century. The *New York Times* editorial of August 28, 1958, characterized Vaughan Williams as a composer of "nine great symphonies — symphonies that, in our age, are unparalleled for sweep, vision and musical imagination. . . . His was a style and an idiom forged from belief, and not capable of imitating or being imitated." This study will deal with the nine symphonies, and, through analysis, with the nature of Vaughan Williams' unique musical style.

It is a curious fact that the symphonies of Ralph Vaughan Williams, which are numbered among the finest musical contributions of the twentieth century, are little known in the United States in comparison to his lighter works. Vaughan Williams is known in this country for his many choral works and the *Greensleeves Fantasia*. The *Fantasia on a Theme of Thomas Tallis* is a staple in the repertoire of many orchestras and is included in the syllabus of many an "appreciation" course. His symphonies are less known and less often heard in the classroom and the concert hall. A major purpose in undertaking these analyses, therefore, is to bring these symphonies to the attention of the student and teacher of music. The *raison d'être* of this project is that the symphonies are worthy of intensive study.

Any serious study — even "appreciation" — of music must be made with a maximum of insight into and understanding of the composer's language, i.e., it must concern itself primarily with structural analysis. Full or systematic analyses have not been made of the nine Vaughan Williams symphonies. Ralph Vaughan Williams creatively outlived all his biographies except two. As each new book or monograph about the composer appeared during the last decade, a new Vaughan Williams composition appeared which in part contradicted previously published theories of the nature of his musical style. Hubert Foss's fine study, written in 1950, refers to the first six symphonies; Frank Howes's work of 1954 includes reference to the seventh symphony, the *Sinfonia Antartica*. Each appeared to be definitive at the time of its publication. Two major books about Vaughan Williams have appeared since the composer's death: James Day's biography of 1961 and A. E. F. Dickinson's extensive study of 1963, both of which refer to all nine symphonies. Like the Foss and Howes studies, these are addressed to a large listening public. But since the four works are designed to be read by laymen, the analyses of the symphonies are necessarily incomplete; they function as program notes rather than as guides to musical structure.[1]

In contrast, this study is addressed to professional musicians and to all concerned with the serious study of musical analysis. In the analyses of the nine Vaughan Williams symphonies, several factors are considered: 1) Technical elements, which include form, melody, harmony, counterpoint, rhythm and orchestration. 2) The "content," or the composer's personal, expressive objectives. These objectives are related in turn to social, cultural and personal factors, and are expressed in terms of the technical elements cited above. 3) The significant influences of previous techniques and esthetics which contribute to the evolution of an individual composer's style.

The need for stylistic analysis has often been stressed; in a book of this sort the arguments in support of such analysis need not be repeated. The reader will note, however, that the advantages derived from the study and practice of analysis apply to the young composer and performer as well as to the theory student. The recognition and appreciation of "style"

and the structural components of that style are essential factors in intelligent performance; similarly, the composer may
learn a great deal about his own distinctive musical personality
by examining the unique ways in which other individuals have
expressed themselves. Moreover, the increased importance
of analysis in the understanding of contemporary music is, or
should be, self-evident. This study of the symphonies of
Ralph Vaughan Williams is presented in three parts: 1) an
outline of the current musical traditions in England when
Vaughan Williams began his career as a symphonist; 2) an
analysis of each of the nine symphonies, with reference to its
significant technical and structural aspects; 3) an analysis of
Vaughan Williams' musical style and its relevance to the
question of meaning in music.

The general orientation of this study follows Ernest Newman's contention that the elements of a composer's style are
related functionally to his esthetic purposes. Although all
composers working within the mainstream of the eighteenth
and nineteenth century tradition (and Vaughan Williams was,
to a great degree, a traditionalist) have used a common language, each composer has developed a unique personal rhe-
toric, a divergence from the norm — his own style, or expressive language. The most important purpose of analysis is the
recognition of these personal elements, the points at which
the composer departs from common practice and follows his
own instincts.

It may be argued that such analysis is not analysis at all,
that it describes but does not explain musical structure. To
reply briefly: the method of analysis outlined above attempts
to explain musical structure esthetically (in terms of expressive symbols) but *not* structurally (in terms of a super-
structure which determines all components). To undertake
the latter form of analysis, one must assume that the art of
music is more rational than perhaps it really is (the Post-
Webernian music of our own age excepted). The present
analyses, then, will follow the English tradition rather than
the German, the descriptive-cognitive approach of Tovey,

Deryck Cooke's concept of music as an expressive "language," and Newman's belief that there is a "physiology" of style peculiar to every composer: "By a 'physiology' of a composer I mean an analysis of his mind not so much in respect of what it has done but of how it works. . . . I have come to the conclusion that, stylistically, each of [the composers] proceeds unconsciously on a few basic formulae."[2] The present study represents an attempt to discover these formulae.

Many friends and colleagues have stimulated my thinking on the works of Vaughan Williams. I am especially grateful to the late Howard A. Murphy, who was vitally involved in the origins and early stages of this study, and to Charles Walton, Robert Pace, and Ernest Harris, all of Columbia University. Robert Barrows of Williams College offered many helpful suggestions. Deserving of special thanks are Leone A. Barron of the University of Massachusetts Press, my good friend and fellow composer Barney Childs, and my wife, who has provided not only the portrait of Vaughan Williams for the frontispiece, but encouragement, sympathy, and patience.

ELLIOTT S. SCHWARTZ

Acknowledgments

The author is grateful to the following publishers for permission to use quotations or music examples from works published or controlled by them.

G. Schirmer, Inc.: *Pastoral Symphony,* by Ralph Vaughan Williams, copyright 1924 by J. Curwen & Sons Ltd.

By permission of Stainer and Bell, Ltd., Sole Agent, Galaxy Music Corporation: *A Sea Symphony,* copyright 1926; *A London Symphony,* copyright 1920, by Ralph Vaughan Williams.

Oxford University Press, Inc.: *Ralph Vaughan Williams — A Study,* by Hubert Foss, copyright 1950; *The Music of Ralph Vaughan Williams,* by Frank Howes, copyright 1954; and the following works by Ralph Vaughan Williams: *Symphony in F minor,* copyright 1935; *Symphony in D major,* copyright 1946; *Symphony in E minor,* copyright 1948; *Sinfonia Antartica,* copyright 1953; *Symphony No. 8 in D minor,* copyright 1956; *Symphony No. 9 in E minor,* copyright 1958.

Contents

FRONTISPIECE

Portrait of Ralph Vaughan Williams
by Dorothy Feldman

PART ONE

THE HISTORICAL
CONTEXT

The English Musical Tradition

Vaughan Williams recovers contact with our cultural tradition
at precisely the point in the seventeenth century when it disin-
tegrated. He shows us, not perhaps what we are or can be,
but what we might have been.

Wilfrid Mellers, *Romanticism and the Twentieth Century*

WE ARE ALL FAMILIAR WITH the literature of the symphonic
tradition, the gradual evolution of the symphonic form from
its beginnings in the Baroque era to the late nineteenth century works of Brahms, Tchaikowsky, Bruckner. From this literature evolved the concept of symphony as it may have appeared to a young composer in the early years of this century.
Ralph Vaughan Williams had to approach the problem of the
symphony with some notion of its traditions, demands and
limitations. However, as an English composer, he was also
well aware of the English tradition of composition and the
peculiar problems inherent in that tradition. Most important, he must have realized that the English tradition and
the European symphonic tradition were at odds.

It is curious that England had, by the year 1900, contributed so little to the musical developments of the preceding
two centuries. English composers not only withdrew from
the mainstream of the European tradition but were unable to
develop a distinctly national idiom. What little they absorbed
of continental culture served only to stifle their own growth;
they preferred to imitate rather than assimilate. The English
musicians of the eighteenth and nineteenth centuries seemed
unaware of a national heritage and unwilling to build one,
while the English public manifested a "curious partiality for

3

the musical traditions of any nation but its own."[1] The period was characterized by the importation of foreign composers and virtuosi and the adoption by English composers of native innovations only after they had been assimilated on the continent and imported back to England. There were, of course, exceptions. The great names of Dunstable, Byrd, Gibbons and Purcell ornament the history of music from the thirteenth through the seventeenth centuries. Yet even during this "Golden Age" certain foibles appeared which were to contribute to the later decline of English music.

John Dunstable (d. 1453) was one of the few English composers to build on native tradition, one of the first English composers of whom we have record, and certainly the first great name in English music. Dunstable traveled abroad, and many of his musical ideas were absorbed by his continental contemporaries, Dufay and Binchois. Specifically, the old English practice of "gymel," or use of parallel organum in thirds, which dated from the late twelfth or early thirteenth century, was adopted by the Netherlanders.[2] The technique was well suited to the new concept of sonority that was replacing the more austere sounds of the French *ars antiqua*. However, Dunstable's English successors failed to build upon his accomplishments, and English music did not keep pace with the developments of the Franco-Flemish school to which Dunstable had contributed. English composers were reluctant to abandon the cantus, and years passed before they made use of the technique of imitative counterpoint, which finally became widespread during the reign of Henry VIII. But by this time they had become followers (of Josquin and Ockeghem) rather than leaders in musical development.

Nevertheless, the reign of Henry VIII was an active one musically. Certain composers rose to prominence, among them those whom Eric Blom calls the "three T's": Thomas Tallis, John Taverner and Christopher Tye.[3] Henry was one of the first English monarchs to bring foreign musicians to his court, and his English court musicians traveled abroad with him. Foreign influences were absorbed and used in a thoroughly English way. The use of Flemish techniques resulted in the "anthems" for the Church of England, and the Italian madrigal was converted into the English madrigal.

This intense musical activity does not minimize the fact that English music was little known and appreciated on the continent. Leichtentritt suggests three reasons for the decline of England's musical position abroad: the belief that the English musical style was largely imitative; the language barrier, since both sacred and secular music were set to English texts; and the fact that England was the last of the great nations to begin printing music.[4]

During the latter half of the sixteenth century, roughly corresponding to the reign of Elizabeth I, music flourished. The English madrigal became perfected, the anthem was popular, and much was written for the virginal. The composers of the time include William Byrd, Orlando Gibbons, John Bull, John Dowland, Thomas Weelkes and John Wilbye. Although the Elizabethan period was one of extensive assimilation of foreign culture, particularly the French and Italian, it contributed much in its own right to the formation of the European Baroque instrumental style. It was certainly one of the most fruitful periods in English music.

The growth of English music came to a sudden end, however, early in the seventeenth century. Charles I, who ascended the throne in 1625, had limited musical tastes. He demanded music of a lively nature, masques for the entertainment of his court. The madrigal was neglected and declined during his reign. The Cromwell government which followed, opposed to all that Charles had stood for, determined to eliminate anything that might have served the cause of revelry and carnality. As Blom states, "Cromwell himself was fond of music. . . . However, [his] Puritan zeal went so much farther than his musical enthusiasm that when the two interests clashed, as they were bound to do in church matters, music had to yield."[5]

Music fared no better under the Restoration monarch, Charles II, who seized the throne in 1660. Charles had been educated in France, where he had acquired a taste for everything French. He was determined to model his court after that of Louis XIV, complete in every extravagant detail. As a result, Charles demanded his own version of the *ballet de cour* and populated his court with foreign musicians. Promising English musicians were sent abroad for further study. "In 1664 . . . Humfrey at seventeen was sent to Paris by the king, to be turned, as Pepys disgustedly remarked three years later, 'into an absolute Monsieur, as full of form, and confidence, and vanity.' "[6] As Walker describes the period, "the main feature of the whole of the music of the Restoration is the emergence of the art into the full atmosphere of secularity and publicity . . . gradually there becomes visible the pressure on a composer to write to satisfy someone else more primarily than himself."[7]

The increasing hold of the English public over the composer became evident in the failure of English opera. Unfortunately, English composers and librettists had made a concerted effort towards a national music drama at precisely the moment when the public craze for foreign opera was beginning. Tentative steps had been made in the direction of English opera throughout the greater part of the century. The masques favored by Charles I had included elements of declamatory and lyric song. When the Cromwell government restricted all forms of entertainment, it still tolerated the masque, since the medium served well as a vehicle for moral and noble sentiments. Surviving the scathing years of the Cromwellian regime, the masque entered the Restoration period at a comparatively mature state of development. The numerous attempts at a more complex form of musical drama during the latter half of the seventeenth century justify the belief that English opera would have developed had it received any support. However, audiences were perfectly satisfied with native drama and foreign opera.[8]

Henry Purcell was the one figure of the period gifted enough to withstand the forces of foreign musical domination. He absorbed both native and foreign strains into his personal idiom, a standard procedure during the Restoration but one rarely used with such taste or imagination. Although he worked within the conventions and constraints of his time, he transformed them into a distinctly English musical style. Elements of the English anthems and songs, Italian chamber music, and French and Italian opera appear in his works, which are unmatched for versatility or variety by any other composer of the time.[9] His opera, *Dido and Aeneas,* was to stand for two centuries as England's only major contribution to the medium. Had Purcell not died in 1695 at the age of thirty-six, and had other English composers been capable of carrying his work forward, a native musical tradition might have emerged.

J. A. Fuller Maitland, referring to the late nineteenth century in England, states that "the vogue of exotic opera — that is, opera in a foreign tongue — has always accompanied a period of artistic sterility in music."[10] His observation is equally applicable to the England of the early eighteenth century; it is all the more appropriate because the sterility had its real beginnings in this earlier era. The passion for French music fostered by Charles II had waned, and both the court of Queen Anne and the public clamored for Italian opera.

In 1710, a twenty-five-year-old German composer of Italian opera, determined to beat other foreigners at their own game, arrived in London at the invitation of the Duke of Manchester. One must agree with Blom that "with the possible exception of Wagner, Handel is music's greatest opportunist."[11] The Birthday Ode which he wrote for the Queen in 1712 won him a yearly pension, and the *Te Deum* written on the occasion of the Peace of Utrecht won him the everlasting adulation of the English people. He wrote Italian opera only as long as it was popular; when he saw it beginning to wane, he quickly dropped it in favor of a new form.

The growing reaction to Italian opera had resulted in the production of *The Beggar's Opera* in 1728. A collection of the favorite tunes of the day, set to a libretto by John Gay, it ridiculed many of the conventions of Italian opera and contributed to its decline. (However, as Leichtentritt points out, the irony of the situation lay in the fact that without the aid of a German, John Christopher Pepusch, who arranged most of the music and wrote the overture, this parody of foreign opera could not have been launched.[12]) When, by 1737, Italian opera had lost much of its appeal, Handel seized upon the idea of the oratorio. He directed his expression to the great English masses, especially to the sturdy middle class. There were few really "English" elements in the oratorio as conceived by Handel and imitated by succeeding English generations. Although the starting points were the English anthem and the English text of the Old Testament, Handel added the dramatic flourishes and highly emotional qualities of Italian opera, plus a unique power and drive that was unmistakably German.

It is impossible to estimate the extent of the damage done to English music through the influence of Handel.[13] This influence, which lasted for a century until Mendelssohn gave the *coup de grâce* to native music, stifled native creativity and prevented English composers from assimilating foreign musical developments. English composers of Handel's time and after his death were quite content to write in the Handelian idiom, which is extremely easy to imitate. Any respectable composer, well-schooled if lacking in talent, can (and did) manufacture stylistically correct pseudo-Handel, completely lacking the power and spirit of the original. Moreover, Handel's influence was stifling because his style led to nothing really new. Handel himself represented the end of an age, even more so than his contemporary, J. S. Bach. Mellers notes that

Bach's crucial position in European musical history consists in the manner in which the old Catholic vocal polyphony, the new Protestant harmonized declamation, and the new dance shapes meet in his work, with the operatic "da capo" aria . . . midway between. Bach includes the past and much of the future. Handel, at his Italianate best, is *par excellence* the composer of the late baroque. . . . Bach is that and much more.[14]

The shackles of the Handelian tradition were so strong that English composers were deaf to European developments which led to the growth of the sonata and symphony. Having to contend with the powerful and conservative public, whose tastes still reflected their love of Handel, the composers dared not trifle with new forms. They dutifully produced a great deal of choral and instrumental music in the Handelian idiom and nothing in the sonata form. Had they strayed from the beaten paths, they would have met with nothing but scorn. Thomas Roseingrave, a contemporary of Handel who had dared to attempt music in the idiom of Purcell and D. Scarlatti, was denounced as roundly as Charles Ives was in the early years of this century. Oddly enough, the English knew of foreign developments, as shown by Haydn's two invitations to London, but by this time were unable to respond to them. Noting the frequent London performances of Haydn and Mozart, Mellers concludes that "we were unable to assimilate their dramatic implications; hence the legend of the 'childlike' Mozart and 'old Papa' Haydn." [15]

During the first half of the nineteenth century, composers such as Samuel Wesley (1810-1876) continued to write in the Handelian tradition, concentrating their efforts on sacred choral music. The period that produced such giants as Schubert, Schumann, Chopin and Berlioz was a thoroughly uncreative one in England. Since by this time composers had lost contact both with their own native idiom and with the important developments on the Continent, their style grew progressively more and more imitative of the more reactionary tendencies in Europe as well as of the Handelian tradition.

The most important post-Handelian influence was the music of Felix Mendelssohn. The premiere of *Elijah* at Birmingham in 1846 was the greatest success of Mendelssohn's career, and when he died one year later, the English musical world was stunned. Mendelssohn had, in fact, made such an impact upon the English that, in the years immediately following his death, his music was accorded a reverence reserved usually for the Masters. Mendelssohn and Handel thus became the models, the standards by which the English public judged native music. Sir William Sterndale Bennett (1816-1875) was a typically Victorian product of this influence; showing promise as a youth, he was sent abroad, studied

under Mendelssohn, and became a miniature Mendelssohn —
a composer of innocuous choral pieces and concert overtures.
It is significant that Mendelssohn's works appealed so strongly
to the Victorian taste. They were ideally suited to the Victorian standards of grace, delicacy, domesticity. In one sense,
the music was as polished, "correct," and relatively lifeless as
the society that embraced it.

England's darkest musical era came to an end, however,
late in the nineteenth century. A new generation of composers
had reached maturity, among them Cowen, Mackenzie, Parry,
and Stanford. Their outlook was strikingly different from
that of earlier generations. Highly intelligent and well
schooled in all the arts, they were intensely aware of the
European developments that had taken place during England's musical slumbers. They turned their attention to the
orchestra, realizing that the English composer must come to
grips with the problem of the symphony. These men did not
consider themselves nationalists; they drew their materials
from many sources. However, in the course of their re-
search, they studied the English madrigals, anthems, and instrumental works of the Tudor and Restoration eras. The
interest in the English musical tradition was heightened by
Cecil Sharp's study and collection of folk music.[16]

Two other English composers sought an escape from the
cul-de-sac through a conscious alliance with the symphonic tradition of the German romantics. Elgar (1857-1934) and
Delius (1862-1934) approached this tradition in different
ways, however, because of their antithetic personalities. Delius, a sensitive introvert, wrote refined, sensuous, subjective
music of an impressionistic nature. In contrast, Elgar, a musical extrovert, approached large orchestral and choral forms
with his audience in mind. Perhaps Delius and Elgar, in their
alliance with a foreign tradition, do not represent a new
strength in English music. It is indisputable, however, that
their music is symptomatic of a new set of goals. English
composers had finally determined to overcome the timidity and
reluctance in handling large symphonic forms which had
characterized their music for over a century.

The Education of Vaughan Williams

IN DISCUSSING the important events in the musical career of Ralph Vaughan Williams before the first performance of *A Sea Symphony* in 1910, one must consider the varied influences that shaped his development. These extend back beyond Parry and Stanford — in fact, beyond Purcell. Moreover, his formative years extend into the last period of his life — his artistic growth never ceased. His formal education is not the clue to his development; the education of a truly creative man is only partly formal. Most of it is informal, far-reaching, cumulative and never-ending.

Ralph Vaughan Williams was born on October 12, 1872, the son of the Rev. Arthur Vaughan Williams, Rector of Down Ampey, Gloucestershire, England. The exact age at which he was introduced to music cannot be determined, either by Vaughan Williams or his biographers. However, the composer does remember his first original composition, a piano piece written at the age of six. He studied theory with the help of his aunt. At the age of seven he began the study of the violin, "which was my musical salvation."[1] It is worth noting that Vaughan Williams is one of the few great composers who was not primarily a pianist. He did not enjoy the piano, wrote sparingly for it, and showed a surprising lack of sensitivity to its resources. But he became a competent violinist; at Charterhouse, from which he graduated in 1890, he played second violin and viola in the school orchestra.

Early in his studies he discovered the music of J. S. Bach, which impressed him greatly. "Of Bach I then knew nothing, and I imagined vaguely that he was like Handel but not so good. This Bach album was a revelation . . . and Bach still remains for me in a niche by himself." Note the reference to Handel, still the staple of every English child's musical diet. "Handel, Mozart, Haydn, and some early Beethoven was what we were fed on at home. My brother, sister and I were encouraged to play pianoforte duets from funny old volumes containing choruses from *Messiah* and *Israel*. . . ." The great love for Bach not only exerted a strong influence *per se* upon Vaughan Williams, but also served as an antidote for the Handelian influence.

Vaughan Williams studied at the Royal College of Music until 1892, working in composition under Parry.

I had first heard of Parry some years before, when I was still a schoolboy. I remember my cousin . . . coming into the room full of that new book *Studies of Great Composers*. "This man Parry," he said, "declares that a composer must write music as his conscience demands." That was quite a new idea to me, the loyalty of the artist to his art.

In 1892 he went to Trinity College, Cambridge, and received his Mus. Bac. degree in 1894 and B.A. in 1895. Here he studied composition and organ, and conducted a small choral group. In 1895, he returned to the Royal College of Music, where he studied composition with Stanford. He accepted a post as organist at South Lambert Church and later (1901) received his doctorate in music from Cambridge. His formal education was complete.

But during his student days Vaughan Williams had acquired a more informal kind of education. In the summer of 1890 he had visited Munich, heard Wagner and, by his own admission, been overwhelmed. He was in Bayreuth in 1896, and in 1897 went to Berlin not only to study at the Akademie der Kunst under Max Bruch, but because "Berlin was the only town at that time where they performed *The Ring* without cuts!" Upon his return to England, he applied for study with Sir Edward Elgar, who politely refused. Undaunted, Vaughan Williams undertook a diligent study of Elgar's larger orchestral works. In 1903 he began to collect folk songs; a year later he joined the English Folk Song Society. By 1905 he was already working "in the field," collecting folk songs in Norfolk.[2] He had also begun work on what was later to become *A Sea Symphony*.

These were the years when the influence of Mendelssohn and the Victorian tradition began to wane. In 1904 Vaughan Williams was asked to edit a new edition of the English Hymnal, in an effort to break down this tradition in one important area of England's musical life. He readily accepted the offer, for the project had a two-fold appeal: the study of English melody was closely related to his investigation of folk song, and he would be obliged to make artistic arrangements of these songs, as his idol Bach had done with Lutheran chorales. In his own words, "I know now that two years of close association with some of the best — as well as some of the worst — tunes in the world was a better musical education than any amount of sonatas and fugues."[3]

Upon the advice of friends, Vaughan Williams went to Paris in 1908 to study with Maurice Ravel. Disagreement still exists as to the extent of Ravel's influence, but it is certain that the sessions spent with Ravel made an impression on Vaughan Williams. "I learnt much from him. For example, that the heavy contrapuntal Teutonic manner was not necessary. . . . It was an invigorating experience to find all artistic problems looked at from what was to me an entirely new angle."

In Vaughan Williams' opinion, one of the greatest influences on his development was the friendship begun in 1895 with a classmate named Gustav Holst. The friendship continued until Holst's death in 1934. Like Vaughan Williams, Holst was an ambitious young composer, seriously concerned with the development of a native English style and blessed with an honest attitude toward his own efforts.[4] Of their conversations, Vaughan Williams wrote, "On these occasions we would devote a whole day, or at least an afternoon, to examining each other's compositions . . . they continued to the end — that is to say, for nearly forty years."

Parry, Stanford, the English Hymnal, Bach, the English

folk song, Wagner, Holst, Bruch, Ravel — these were some of the elements that contributed to Vaughan Williams' early growth. It was characteristic of his nature that he should mature slowly, by steps and not by bounds. He was not considered a distinguished student in school or in college, but he was an alert and thoughtful one. His honesty of approach, as seen in his critical sessions with Holst, may account for his slow and careful development. In A. E. F. Dickinson's words, "he is one of the most downright composers that ever lived. . . . His continual revision of past work is the sign . . . of increasing determination to know himself — which, after all, is the chief business of living."[5]

In one sense, the early years represent Vaughan Williams' initial attempts at getting to know himself. When in 1910 his first major works, *A Sea Symphony* and the *Fantasia on a Theme of Tallis,* were produced, the composer had reached the age of thirty-eight. Purcell was dead at thirty-six, Mozart at thirty-five, Schubert at thirty-one. Vaughan Williams' initial creative stage was, admittedly, a lengthy one. But in the light of his later growth, there can be no denying that it was a strong foundation.

PART TWO

THE NINE SYMPHONIES

A Note on the Procedure of Analysis

Each symphony is analyzed individually with respect to its important stylistic characteristics (melody, harmony, etc.), although these are discussed here only in the context of the larger analysis of the form of each movement.

Readers *primarily* concerned with the elements of melody, harmony, counterpoint, rhythm, orchestration and tonality as they function within the symphonic style of Vaughan Williams will find these treated more extensively in Part III of this volume.

An Overview of the Symphonies

IN EXAMINING THE NINE SYMPHONIES of Ralph Vaughan
Williams, one is immediately struck by the fact that no two
of them are alike, either in structure or in mood. This amazing variety encompasses the grandiosity and majesty of the
Sea and *London* Symphonies, the tranquillity and understatement of the *Pastoral Symphony,* the violence of the Fourth
Symphony, the contemplative mysticism of the Fifth Symphony, the humor and high spirits of the Eighth Symphony.
Each new work appeared as something of an incongruity, a
deviation from the accepted norm, even to those who were
well acquainted with the composer's preceding works. It is no
wonder that musicians eventually came to expect the unexpected from Ralph Vaughan Williams.

Perhaps the most overwhelming fact to be considered, certainly the most unusual, is the enormous time span covered by
the symphonies. From *A Sea Symphony* (1910) to the Ninth
Symphony (1958), the listener must traverse nearly half a
century of musical creativity, all the more amazing when one
recalls that Vaughan Williams was thirty-eight years old
when he completed *A Sea Symphony,* a rather late start by
any standards. When the composer had completed the *Pastoral Symphony,* third of the nine, he had reached the age
of fifty, and, at sixty-three, when the Fourth Symphony appeared, he was already considered the Grand Old Man of
English music. The last five of the nine, therefore, were composed within the last twenty years of Vaughan Williams' long
life. Rarely has an artist been so prolific in his seventies and
eighties; the only comparable feat, to this writer's knowledge,
is the completion of *Falstaff* by Giuseppe Verdi at the age

17

of seventy-nine. Charles Ives, Richard Strauss and Jan Sibelius, in our own time, were blessed with long life but were
comparatively unproductive in their later years.

The symphonies can be divided into three distinct groups,
each containing three works. The first three of the nine
symphonies are *A Sea Symphony, A London Symphony* and
the *Pastoral Symphony.* These works, composed between
1910 and 1922, are directly related to life; more specifically,
they are related to aspects of English life, and reflect Vaughan
Williams' nationalistic orientation during this period. *A Sea
Symphony* is the most literally programmatic of the three;
written for vocal soloists, chorus and orchestra, it is set to
poetry of Walt Whitman, and is therefore specific in its references. *A London Symphony* is less programmatic and more
impressionistic in its intent, attempting to represent the
sounds, moods and character of the city rather than a literal
description of it. The *Pastoral Symphony* is even less literal
than *A London Symphony,* portraying the quiet and contemplative character associated with the countryside, but
nothing more specific than this.

As noted, more than a dozen years elapsed before the appearance of the Fourth Symphony in 1935. The Fourth, Fifth
and Sixth Symphonies, composed between 1935 and 1948, are
not programmatic in the sense of the first three, but are related to the critical World War II period during which they
were written. These three symphonies are the most powerful
and expressive of the nine, and any reaction to them in terms
of actual events of the time of their composition, although
not specifically indicated by the composer, would seem legiti-
mate. Critics and audiences have interpreted the Fourth
Symphony as an angry, violent reaction to (or portrayal of)
the rise of Fascism in Europe. The Fifth Symphony, similarly, has been directly related to the period of its composition. Written in 1942 at the height of the war, it is
surprisingly optimistic, affirmative, even religious in its allusions to hymns and to the writings of Bunyan. The work, in
fact, served as a musical rallying point for the besieged Eng-

lish people; it was performed extensively and heard on the radio by many. The Sixth Symphony, written after the conclusion of the war, is anything but affirmative. The work may represent a reaction to the war, or perhaps disillusionment with the peace; at any rate, it is a highly dramatic symphony, and its famous finale — a slow, seemingly aimless flux, pianissimo throughout — is especially provocative.

The last three symphonies, written between 1952 and 1958, are not so weighty as the Fourth, Fifth and Sixth. The *Sinfonia Antartica* of 1952 is an adaptation of music written by Vaughan Williams for a film dealing with the unsuccessful Scott Expedition to the Antarctic. The *Sinfonia,* essentially a suite of five contrasting movements, retains references to the Scott expedition. Each of the movements is, in fact, prefaced by a short literary quotation which sets the stage for the music that follows, much of which is programmatic in its allusions. The Eighth Symphony is the most humorous of the nine, a short, highly entertaining piece in which various movements are assigned to individual "families" of the orchestra. The Ninth Symphony, completed shortly before the composer's death in 1958, is a work of many sharp contrasts and is in certain respects reminiscent of the preceding symphonies.

These final symphonies, written between the composer's eightieth and eighty-sixth years, demonstrate his seemingly perpetual freshness of approach and outlook; new techniques are explored, unusual instruments are employed, and an almost youthful exuberance is evident in many passages. They are a testimony to the remarkable capacity for change and creative growth that characterized Ralph Vaughan Williams.

A Sea Symphony

VAUGHAN WILLIAMS' FIRST SYMPHONY was a choral one, scored for baritone and soprano soloists, chorus and orchestra. There are two probable reasons for his choice of this medium. The first of these is related directly to the composer's natural inclination toward vocal composition. It will be recalled that Vaughan Williams began his musical career by editing the English Hymnal and collecting folk songs. Until the year 1910, the majority of his compositions had been vocal or choral, in the English tradition that extended from the Elizabethans to Stanford and Parry. Secondly, through the outlet of the great English Festivals, the young composer's choice of the choral medium for his more ambitious works increased the possibility of performance and public recognition. It was the Leeds Festival which had sponsored the first performance, in 1907, of *Toward the Unknown Region* and which produced *A Sea Symphony* in 1910.

It is noteworthy that both of these choral works are set to poems of Walt Whitman. Vaughan Williams was strongly attracted to Whitman, particularly to certain tendencies that are paralleled in his own music: the concern for the development of a national art independent of foreign influences and the recurring theme of mysticism and exploration, which is related to Transcendentalism.[1] His affinity to Whitman notwithstanding, however, he altered the original text for use in *A Sea Symphony,* deleting certain lines and repeating others.[2]

The text of each of the first three movements presents a different aspect of the sea, while that of the last movement unites these varied approaches into a larger, "transcendental" meaning. A. E. F. Dickinson has summarized these textual implications as follows:

20

I. "Behold, the sea itself." Limitless, indomitable. And not less indomitable the sailors, the "unnamed heroes . . . whom fate can never surprise nor death dismay. . . ."

II. So, to the philosophic mind the sea is a vast symbol of all human life.

III. (Descriptive digression.) Look at it! That wonderful panorama of a myriad waves, following the great ship as ceaselessly as they are displaced by it.

IV. *Now I begin to see the meaning of it all.* These restless explorations will lead to a Reality of some kind. . . . "We too take ship, O Soul . . . steer for the deep waters only . . . where mariner has not yet dared to go. . . . O farther, farther sail!"[3]

A cyclic use of three leitmotifs serves to unify the four movements of the symphony. These motives are, in the order of their initial appearance:

A. An harmonic progression, in which a minor triad resolves to a major triad whose root is a major third higher:

Motive A

Mvt. I, m 3-4   Mvt. II, m 1-2

B. A melodic figure which emphasizes the juxtaposition of duplet and triplet rhythmic figures and melodically consists of the rising interval of a third followed by a falling third:

Motive B

C. Another melodic figure, consisting of a repeated-note pattern set in a distinctive rhythm. The pattern also spans the interval of a third:

Motive C

FIRST MOVEMENT

Form	Sonata-Allegro
Exposition	measures 1-220
Development	measures 221-361
Recapitulation	measures 362-401
Coda	measures 402-411

EXPOSITION

Measures 1-16. The work begins with motive A as a brass fanfare, repeated B-flat minor chords resolving into a D major triad. This triad is expanded into a rising arpeggio, which, with the addition of a second and a sixth, outlines a pentatonic scale on D. The first subject is reached at measure 7, a broad melody that contains motive B within itself, built upon a six-tone scale (pentatonic plus leading tone). The fifth and sixth degrees of the scale are emphasized.

Ex. 1

Example 1 is expansively and chromatically treated, as chorus and orchestra dwell on the duple and triple rhythms.

Measures 17-58. A contrasting motive is introduced at measure 17, appearing as an orchestral counterpoint to the choral cries of "see the steamers coming and going." This melody is built upon the same six-tone scale as Ex. 1, and it modulates pentatonically, i.e. from C-sharp major to B-flat major, to A-flat major, and then F-sharp minor.

Ex. 2

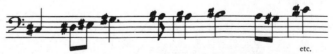

This motive reaches a forceful climax in B-flat minor, which leads back to the opening fanfare, B-flat minor to D major, at measure 42. Example 1 is then broadly stated by both chorus and orchestra and gradually subsides into a quiet passage involving imitation, among solo instruments, of motive B.

Measures 59-126. At measure 59, there is a change of both tempo and mood. The music becomes brisk and lively, indicative of the text's new subject matter: not the "sea itself," but the men and ships that sail it. Moreover, the melodic line has taken on a modal character, through the use of the flatted seventh. After a few bars of light introduction, the baritone soloist makes his first appearance, at measure 67. This theme, the second subject of the movement, contains motive C within it:

Ex. 3

The theme is developed further and taken up by the chorus, involving rapid changes of key center and alternation of mode (Aeolian, Ionian, Mixolydian) characterized by differing inflections of the third and seventh scale degrees.

Measures 127-220. The music's great drive stops suddenly on a held A-flat major triad (second inversion), and the tempo becomes Andante. A new theme is introduced by the baritone soloist; the melody is pentatonic, indirectly related to motive B, and concentrates upon the fifth and sixth scale degrees.

Ex. 4

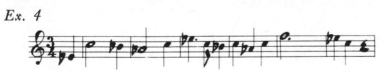

The phrase is immediately restated by the chorus, and the

inflection of the E-flat in the last measure (see above) to an
E-natural results in a modulation to the tonality of C. The
music remains in C from this point, measure 139, until the
end of the exposition. The chant is expanded by both soloist
and chorus in a highly chromatic manner, and a final variant
of Ex. 4 in the minor mode leads to a climax, fortissimo, in
C minor.

DEVELOPMENT

Measures 221-268. The opening brass fanfare, now a series of C minor triads, returns at measure 221, and the soprano soloist makes her initial appearance at measure 223
with the following chant:

Ex. 5

This semirecitative is related to motive C and is repeated by
the chorus, beginning at measure 227. The choral statement
is immediately answered by a fragment of Ex. 1 in the orchestra, and at measure 233 the brass fanfare returns, now a
series of E major triads. Example 5 is repeated, first by
soprano solo and then by chorus, again answered by a fragment of Ex. 1 which dissolves into a rapidly descending scale
passage.

A tempo change at measure 241 marks the beginning of
an extended passage for soprano and chorus, built upon the
inversion of motive B:

The expansion of this material is based upon repeated se-

quences and the continual use of secondary dominant-tonic
relationships. A chromatically descending bass line is introduced at measure 257, and the music builds in intensity. The
passage reaches a climax at measure 264, then subsides on a
quiet cadence in D major at measure 268.

Measures 269-345. The alto section of the chorus enters
at measure 269 with a soft statement of Ex. 2, answered
fugally by the sopranos at measure 274, tenors at measure
278 and basses at measure 282. The expansion of this material is again sequential and employs the dominant-tonic relationship extensively. A gradual crescendo leads to a climax at
measure 298, and a variant of Ex. 2 is introduced by the altos
at measure 302, again treated fugally and developed as an
extended crescendo built upon sequences. The music increases
in tempo at measure 320, continuing animatedly to a fortissimo at measure 345.

Measures 345-362. Another variant of Ex. 2, introduced
by the basses at measure 345, is imitated throughout the
chorus, as the passage continues to build in volume. Beginning at measure 352, the tonic D major is approached through
an expansion of a repeated B-flat minor triad, i.e. an expansion of motive A.

The passage reaches a great climax, triple forte, at measure 358, and rapidly subsides until the tonic triad is reached,
pianissimo, at measure 362.

RECAPITULATION

Measures 362-401. Only the first subject proper, Ex. 1, is
treated in the Recapitulation. This deviation may have been
in part due to the nature of the text. The continuity of the
poem thus remains unbroken, which might have been difficult
had formal "balance" been adhered to in the musical setting.

A quiet ostinato pattern in high strings and woodwinds is
established in measure 362, over which the baritone soloist
enters (measure 365) with Ex. 1. A fragment of the theme
is imitated alternately by baritone and chorus, leading to the

entrance of the soprano soloist at measure 379. A crescendo
leads to a broad orchestral statement of Ex. 1 in its complete
form at measure 384, serving as a countersubject to the choral
chant of "One flag above all the rest."

A sudden shift from the D major tonic to a C minor triad
at measure 391 marks the return of the text "behold the sea
itself" in the chorus and motive B in the low winds. The C
minor pedal point, in low tremolo strings, continues under a
soprano solo statement of the text, and then subsides to a
low tremolo F-sharp at measure 401.

CODA

Measures 402-411. Over the held F-sharp pedal point, the
chorus, divided into eight parts, chants "all seas, all ships"
upon a pentatonic D scale, eventually fading into silence upon
a held tonic triad.

SECOND MOVEMENT

Form	Ternary
Section A	measures 1-53
Section B	measures 54-135
Section A'	measures 136-172

SECTION A

Measures 1-53. The movement begins with an orchestral
statement of motive A, consisting of alternating C minor and
E major triads, eventually resolving in E minor. At measure
18 the baritone soloist enters with a quiet monotone statement
(on a repeated note E) of the phrase "On the beach at night
alone," over a quiet orchestral figure in E minor, Aeolian
mode.

The altos answer in a similar monotone on the note E, and
at measure 27 an orchestral figure is introduced under another
baritone monotone.

Ex. 1

Note the rising and falling interval of the third, which indicates a relationship to motive C. The theme is taken up by the chorus at measure 29, and a fragment of it is repeated sequentially. Another monotone statement by the soloist, over a melodic figure heard earlier in the movement (see measures 6-11), leads to a quiet restatement of motive A, again C minor to E major, at measure 49.

SECTION B

Measures 54-99. The statement of motive A, noted above, leads directly into the second main section of the movement, as the C minor triad resolves into the tonality of E-flat major. Horns enter with a slow, quiet melody at measure 54.

Ex. 2

This theme is directly related to motive C in its use of repeated tones and the interval of the third. It continues as an ostinato figure, and the baritone enters above it at measure 60.

Ex. 3

The theme is pentatonic, and contains the pattern of motive

B within itself. Examples 2 and 3 are simultaneously expanded and developed, moving from the tonality of E-flat into G major at measure 67 and reaching a climax in A major at measure 81, which subsides gradually. At measure 85 a thematic fragment, first sung by the baritone, is developed sequentially and with chromatic alterations, concluding on a C minor triad at measure 99.

Measures 99-135. Another variant of motive C appears at measure 99, played in the orchestra. The soloist and chorus answer with the phrase "All nations, all identities," also emphasizing repeated tones.

Ex. 4

The tonality shifts to G minor at measure 107, and repeated note G's sung by the chorus suddenly expand into an E-flat major triad at measure 118, followed by a fortissimo orchestral statement of Ex. 4. Choral declamations alternate with Ex. 4, both still fortissimo, the tonality descending by a minor third with each sequence, i.e. from E-flat major to C major to A major. The resolution from C to A majors is repeated, triple forte, by full orchestra, measures 128-130, and subsides upon the *inversion* of motive A, i.e. C minor triads alternating with A major triads (a minor third *below* C). Finally, at measure 136, the C minor resolves a minor third above, to E major.

SECTION A'

Measures 136-172. At a change in inflection from E major to E minor, the baritone repeats his monotone E "On the beach at night alone." The remainder of the movement is entirely orchestral. Example 2 appears at measure 148, and is briefly developed, subsiding on a pianissimo fragment of

Ex. 3 at measure 164 and a very quiet (quadruple piano) E major chord.

THIRD MOVEMENT

Form	Binary (Sonatine)
Exposition	measures 1-212
Interlude	measures 213-274
Recapitulation	measures 275-381

EXPOSITION

Measures 1-130. The movement begins at a brisk tempo (Allegro Brilliante) with a variant of the symphony's opening fanfare on the G minor triad, answered immediately by a choral statement.

Ex. 1

This figure is in itself a type of choral fanfare, rhythmically distinctive and composed of triads moving in skips of thirds.

The music, depicting the "whistling winds" and "myriad waves," is extremely chromatic in part. Note, for example, the rising bass line in the orchestra, measures 20-25. At measure 25 the chorus begins to expand upon a chant-like figure (initially stated at measure 15):

Ex. 2

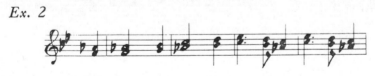

but the choral chant then becomes equally chromatic at measure 33. At measure 42 the tempo is increased, and fragments of the fanfare, Ex. 1, and Ex. 2 are alternated in this highly chromatic harmonic and tonal context. The music builds to a fortissimo at measure 64, and then subsides upon rapidly descending chromatic figures in the orchestra. A march-like figure appears in the low brasses at measure 75, much less chromatic and implying A major. It is sequentially repeated at measure 82 in the area of F-sharp major and again descends a minor third, i.e. to E-flat major, at measure 89.

At measure 90 the chorus introduces another theme, again a chromatic representation of the text:

Ex. 3

etc.

Note the side-slip from the keys of E-flat to E-natural and the highly chromatic treatment of the material that follows, particularly the orchestral passage at measures 104-114. The music suddenly resumes a diatonic character at measure 115, at the words "laughing and buoyant," and there is a direct quotation, at this point in the orchestra, of the folk song "The Golden Vanity."[4] A gradual crescendo leads into the key of B-flat major at measure 130.

Measures 130-212. The tempo is decreased at measure 130, and a broad theme is introduced by both chorus and orchestra.

Ex. 4

etc.

An orchestral ritornello, punctuating each long phrase, is again a direct quotation of a folk song, "The Bold Princess Royal" (see measures 138-139, 148-149). The theme concludes on a rhythmic figure which emphasizes an octave leap from F to F and definitely establishes B-flat major as a diatonic key center, measures 150-170. The final statement of the figure at measure 167 leads, however, to another highly chromatic passage (beginning at measure 170), diminished sevenths chromatically descending in the trombones. The music builds in intensity and leads to a short choral statement of Ex. 1 at measure 209.

INTERLUDE

Measures 213-274. The orchestral interlude begins with an expansion of Ex. 3, moving rapidly through various keys and finally dissolving into a whole-tone passage[5] at measure 252. The rhythmic activity and volume both subside as the whole-tone passage continues, and there is a brief moment of silence.

RECAPITULATION

Measures 275-315. The opening fanfare is again heard, in G minor, and the chorus enters with Ex. 1 at measure 277, briefly expanded. Example 2 immediately follows, beginning at measure 295, and a crescendo built on Ex. 2 resolves, fortissimo, in G major.

Measures 315-381. At a slower tempo, Ex. 4 reappears in the key of G major, and another long crescendo begins, emphasizing the triplet figuration of the fanfare and of Ex. 1 (see measures 344-355). The music reaches a fortissimo at measure 360, in which chords of B-flat major and G major alternate, concluding on three orchestral chords and a final choral cry in G major.

FOURTH MOVEMENT
(in two large sections)

PART I	Sonata-Allegro
Exposition	measures 1-93
Development	measures 93-177
Recapitulation	measures 178-214
Interlude	measures 214-240

PART II   Ternary "Arch" Form[6]
    Section A   measures 241-337
    Section B
        Lento (optional) measures 337-403
        Allegro   measures 403-445
    Section A′   measures 445-540
    CODA   measures 541-571

This movement can almost be considered a complete work in itself, for it contains an opening Sonata-Allegro section, an optional "slow movement" and a "scherzo" passage.[7] This final movement is thus the longest and most complex of the symphony, obviously designed to meet the demands of an equally long and complex text.

PART I — EXPOSITION

Measures 1-93. The movement begins in the key of E-flat major, with a theme stated quietly by chorus and strings.

Ex. 1

The theme is derived from motive B; it is developed lyrically, and at measure 13 moves into the key of G major. E-flat is re-established at measure 23, and at measure 26 a variant of Ex. 1 of movement I is heard in the orchestra and briefly expanded. The music slowly subsides on a choral statement, and there is a brief silence.

At a faster tempo, an orchestral melody appears at measure 51 under a choral monotone on the note D:

Ex. 2

The theme is in the Dorian mode and (in its first four notes) resembles motive C. The material is developed modally, with the addition of a lowered second degree that implies Mixolydian, builds to a climax at measure 85 and then gradually dies down.

DEVELOPMENT

Measures 93-177. At measure 93, motive A is heard softly in the orchestra, appearing as alternating A major and F minor triads. The passage quickly subsides to a fragment of Ex. 2 at measure 101, and then to a very quiet, unaccompanied chorus of altos and sopranos at measure 104. The short *a cappella* passage, meant to be sung offstage, uses parallel progressions of triads in second inversion.[8] After chorus and orchestra build to another climax, the unaccompanied semichorus enters again at measure 126.

This leads directly to a restatement of Ex. 2 at measure 135, stated first by basses and then answered fugally by the other voices. A long crescendo, built upon Ex. 2, leads to a fortissimo in G major and a quickening of tempo at measure 167. G major is repeated again and again, but the music suddenly shifts into E major at measure 178.

RECAPITULATION

Measures 178-214. Example 1 is broadly stated by the brasses in E major at measure 178, and then is heard again in G major at measure 184, leading to a fortissimo choral melisma on the word "singing." This is finally punctuated by short orchestral references to Ex. 2, beginning at measure 203, and a final choral chant on "singing," coming to a definite cadence in G major.

INTERLUDE

Measures 214-240. Motive B is heard in the orchestra at

measure 214, in the key of G, and then moving into the key of E-flat at measure 223. Further elaboration of motive B in E-flat leads directly into the second large part of the finale at measure 241.

PART II — SECTION A

Measures 241-337. There is a sudden crescendo at the end of the Interlude, climaxed by the entrance of the baritone and soprano soloists. The baritone appears first at measure 241 with a broad melody marked "appassionato":

Ex. 3

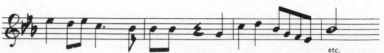

This theme is imitated by the soprano at measure 247. The theme is built upon the six-tone scale (pentatonic plus leading tone) which characterizes those themes derived from motive B. The two soloists engage in a lengthy duet which moves through many key areas, based upon fragments of melody related to motive C (and in one instance joined to a variant of motive B).

Ex. 4

This extended passage is also characterized by the use of sequences and a gradual crescendo which reaches a climax at measure 281 and then subsides. A brief orchestral passage follows, beginning at measure 287, which also employs variants of motive C:

Ex. 5

The baritone enters quietly at measure 300, joined by the soprano at measure 303. Further elaboration of the variants noted in Ex. 4 and Ex. 5, more softly and slowly than before, leads to a restatement of Ex. 3 by the two soloists in canonic imitation (measure 331), and once more in E-flat major. This quiet passage leads directly into the key of C major, and the beginning of the "Lento" section at measure 337.

SECTION B

Measures 337-403. Motive B is heard quietly in the orchestra, and the soloists enter at measure 343 with a short melodic figure.

Ex. 6

The figure is repeated, fortissimo, by the chorus (which has not been heard since measure 214). The figure itself consists of an ascending pentatonic scale. The passage is extended through sequences and builds to a fortissimo at measure 360.

The music suddenly subsides, and the baritone soloist is heard over an ostinato of tremolo chords, alternately C major and minor, then D major-minor. An orchestral passage featuring an ascending melodic line in whole tones (measure 373) leads to a restatement of Ex. 3 by the baritone, measure 376, again in E-flat. The melody is briefly elaborated and then subsides into an orchestral statement of motive B in C major, measure 393.[9] The chorus enters, *a cappella* at measure 398, with Ex. 6, building to a fortissimo at measure 403.

Measures 403-445. The tempo suddenly changes to Allegro, the music is brisk, rhythmic and modal; and the soprano soloist enters with a chant, "Away, O Soul," imitated by the baritone and each choral voice in turn. The passage is characterized by rapidly changing time signatures and by a scale pattern in E-Dorian mode.

Ex. 7

This orchestral pattern serves as a countersubject to the choral cries of "Away . . ." and the music passes from E minor (modal) to C-sharp major and then to B-flat major at measure 426. A gradual crescendo leads to a rushing upward scale passage and a climax at measure 445.

SECTION A'

Measures 445-522. The climax of the rapid scale passage is a held tremolo high D, over which (at a slower tempo) the chorus chants "Sail forth." Fragments previously noted in Ex. 4 are introduced into the orchestral texture at measures 446-447, and 451-452, and a crescendo builds to a restatement of Ex. 5 in both orchestra and chorus, beginning at measure 455. A sudden diminuendo leads into an extended duet for baritone and soprano at a faster tempo, beginning at measure 459, built upon the material of Ex. 4 and then interrupted by a forceful choral version of Ex. 5 at measure 476. Another extended passage for duet, chorus and orchestra based upon Exx. 4 and 5 moves chromatically through many sequences, and builds to a chant of "steer for the deep waters only" (which, as noted in Ex. 4, is related to motive B) at measure

500. This choral chant increases in intensity, and builds to a great climax with Ex. 7 of the "scherzo" section employed as its orchestral countersubject, beginning at measure 505.

The music reaches a triple forte at measure 519, and D major triads are repeated again and again in the orchestra, unexpectedly interrupted by a brief silence at measure 522.

Measures 523-540. The silence is broken by an orchestral statement, pianissimo, of Ex. 3 at a much slower tempo, beginning at measure 523, and in the key of E-flat major. There is a brief expansion of the theme, which fades into a quiet woodwind version of motive B at measures 540-541.

CODA

Measures 541-571. Still at a slow tempo, motive B in the woodwinds alternates with quiet choral cries of "O farther sail," and Ex. 3 reappears in the strings at measure 546. The passage subsides to a quiet close in E-flat, and the music dies away on an open chord of G-E-flat-G in the low register.

❖   ❖   ❖

The reaction to the first performance of *A Sea Symphony* at the Leeds Festival was overwhelmingly favorable. The *London Times* critic wrote, "It will readily be guessed that a composer of such modern tastes has followed no conventional lines in his music, and that it claims rank with that which is newest in the accepted sense." [10]

When viewed in the light of later achievements, the work is not as unconventional as the *Times* critic supposed. Aside from the fine choral writing for which the composer had already become known, the work exhibits a highly eclectic style, an idiom that is not consistent. The composer is, in Young's words, "conscious of many possibilities, but not yet assured in a completely personal mode of expression."[11] The result, in this work, is a fusion of symphony and oratorio, English and Continental, nineteenth and twentieth centuries.

Perhaps the element in this early work typical of the later Vaughan Williams is the ambitious scope of the concept, rather than the music itself. It is reasonable to state that no other Englishman could have attempted anything quite like this work in 1910. Ottaway claims that, even though the piece owes much to the influence of Parry, Parry himself "certainly would not have risen to the occasion . . . his vision was too limited. And Parry's pupil, however much at one with the text, might have easily succumbed to a discursive oratorio style."[12]

Finally, we must realize in retrospect that the diversity of idioms employed in this music must be considered in relation to its equally vast and amorphous text, truly "romantic" in the nineteenth century sense of that term. *A Sea Symphony* thus represents a remarkably bold musical venture, if not a perfect achievement.

A London Symphony

VAUGHAN WILLIAMS' FIRST EXTENDED WORK exclusively for orchestra was *A London Symphony*. It had been preceded by smaller works such as the incidental music to *The Wasps,* the *Fantasia on a Theme by Tallis,* and the *Norfolk Rhapsodies.* With these few exceptions, the music composed before 1914 usually involved the vocal setting of a text.

Foss remarks that "at first the orchestra was for Vaughan Williams an intractable medium; words, on the other hand, did not baffle him."[1] And Vaughan Williams has stated that the concept of a symphony had not occurred to him until his friend and fellow composer George Butterworth suggested it. "At the end of the evening, just as he was getting up to go, he said, in his characteristically abrupt way, 'You know, you ought to write a symphony.' From that moment the idea of a symphony — a thing which I had always declared I would never attempt — dominated my mind."[2]

The work was finished in 1914 and later revised and published in 1920 with a dedication to the memory of Butterworth, who had died in World War I.

FIRST MOVEMENT

Form	Sonata-Allegro
Introduction	measures 1-37
Exposition	measures 38-166
Development	measures 166-287
Recapitulation	measures 288-386
Coda	measures 387-407

INTRODUCTION

Measures 1-30. The symphony begins slowly (Lento) and in the key of G major. The basic structural motive of the entire work is stated in the first two measures. It consists of two intervals of a fourth separated by that of a second:

Ex. 1

A slowly moving counterpoint is established over Ex. 1, and the music proceeds quietly in two-voice polyphony, the upper voice thickened, however, into a succession of triads. Open fifths and chords built in fourths (see measures 8-12, 24-28) also appear in the texture.

Measures 30-37. A short crescendo, beginning at measure 28, is abruptly terminated at measure 30 by a very soft chord emphasizing the intervals of Ex. 1. Over this held chord, harp and clarinet intone the call of London's Big Ben, beginning at measure 31.

Ex. 2

As this "chime" concludes at measure 34, a rhythmic figure develops from the held chord. Beginning in high woodwinds, it accelerates from quarter-note motion to eighths, and then to sixteenths at measure 36. As it continues, a crescendo is built, in which the horns and trumpets proclaim Ex. 1.

EXPOSITION

Measures 38-74. The tempo quickens, and the full orches-

tra states the first motive of the Exposition, triple forte, at
measure 38:

Ex. 3

The opening chord, a triad with an added lowered sixth, is
followed by a descending chromatic movement of minor triads.
The E-flat persists in the bass as a pedal point, over which
minor chords moving in parallel motion appear in low winds
and brass. A new thematic figure is introduced in measure 48
by winds and then answered by brass.

Ex. 4

The interval of the fourth defines the outlines of Ex. 4 and
figures prominently in the theme which immediately follows
it at measure 53:

Ex. 5

A rhythmic bass line in eighth-notes is established at measure
59 against a succession of parallel fifths in low winds and
strings. This pattern develops into an extended melody beginning at measure 63. Example 4 is contained within this
new theme.

Ex. 6

Example 6, the most fully developed melody yet heard, is extended over 12 measures and presented by different orchestral combinations.

Measures 75-111. A short one-measure motive is presented at measure 75, punctuated by parallel chord motion in high winds:

Ex. 7

Through contrapuntal treatment, this thematic figure is extended. At measure 80, the music begins to move from the tonality of G into the key of E-flat, and a figure built upon Ex. 1 (see measure 83) is developed in imitation. Parallel chord motion begins to dominate the texture at measure 95, and a series of minor seventh chords leads to a repetition of Ex. 5, now in the key of B-flat. The lowered sixth, prominent in Ex. 3, has also been added to the texture, and serves as a pedal point, i.e. G-flat in the bass, for an extended crescendo beginning at measure 105.

Measures 112-166. At measure 112, the crescendo reaches its climax on a fortissimo cadential figure:

Ex. 8

The first chord of the progression is a triad with added lowered sixth, as in Ex. 3, and the second chord is built in fourths,
thus related to Ex. 1. After a brief pentatonic phrase in the
strings, Ex. 8 is repeated at measure 117; it is again answered by another brief string passage.

At measure 121 a new theme is introduced by the woodwinds, as the tonality abruptly shifts to A-flat major.

Ex. 9

The melody is pentatonic, and fourths are again outlined in
its contour. It is repeated in G-flat major at measure 128
and leads to still another theme, once more in B-flat, at measure 133:

Ex. 10

Note again the pattern of fourths, related to Ex. 1. Example 10 is presented as a full eight-measure phrase, with a
distinctive countersubject in the higher instruments. At measure 141, the melody is repeated in invertible counterpoint,
so that the two voices have exchanged registers. The music,
which builds to a climax at measure 148, is extended to measure 151 by means of a repeated chord cluster and a rising
brass figure, both built on Ex. 1. At measure 152 Ex. 9 reappears but is quickly interrupted at measure 155 by Ex. 10
in low brasses. A sudden crescendo leads to a full statement,
by low strings, brasses and winds, of Ex. 1. The crescendo
continues, and leads to an abrupt silence at measure 166.

DEVELOPMENT

Measures 166-235. Example 3 appears after the short silence, triple forte and in the key of B-flat. The chromatically descending parallel chords of this motive are elaborated upon, briefly interrupted at measure 178 by Ex. 4 and then followed immediately by a variant of Ex. 1 which had been previously associated with Ex. 10:

This short figure is repeated, and is then extended into a melodic line, beginning at measure 188, which is treated in overlapping imitation by various solo instruments:

Ex. 11

Through this sequential imitation, the tonality shifts to E-flat minor at measure 198, and then into F-sharp minor at measure 202. Example 11 is developed in canonic imitation by strings; this expansion leads to a short rhythmic figure stated by flute at measure 208 and then by bassoon at measure 212. Example 11 is stated by high strings and winds in rhythmic augmentation, beginning at measure 214, interrupted by Ex. 7 in the low register at measures 219 and 222. Example 11 returns at measure 226, again in canonic imitation, subsiding quietly on a held C-sharp in low strings.

Measures 235-287. Two solo 'celli, and then two solo violins, are heard in an ascending scale line, leading into a quiet passage for strings and harp, beginning at measure 239. At a slight increase in tempo, the texture becomes more contrapuntal at measure 254, and then thickened by parallel chord movement. The parallel chord sequences dominate the

texture by measure 270, and a slight crescendo is built, subsiding quickly to a pianissimo at measure 283. A short melodic figure is stated by bassoon, then imitated by solo clarinet,
leading directly into the Recapitulation of the movement.

RECAPITULATION

Measures 288-354. The clarinet solo subsides upon a held
chord, tremolo, of G major plus the added lowered sixth.
Over a held E-flat pedal point, Ex. 3 appears, pianissimo, at
measure 292, followed immediately by reference to Ex. 5
and then Ex. 6. Example 4 is also briefly stated, fortissimo
at measure 308, and a sudden diminuendo leads to a pianissimo brass statement, at measure 311, of Ex. 8.

The prevailing tonality of G abruptly shifts to E major
with the return of Ex. 9 at measure 321, but G major, which
is again resumed by measure 324, leads directly into a pianissimo statement of Ex. 10 in G minor, beginning at measure
330. A sudden crescendo leads to a restatement of Ex. 10
in the major mode, fortissimo, imitated in augmentation:

etc.

This passage is extended through sequences, moving into E
major and then A-flat major, as another crescendo is built.

Measures 355-386. The music becomes suddenly quiet at
measure 355, and Ex. 1 is presented over a moving bass line,
once more in the key of G major. A gradual crescendo, beginning at measure 363, emphasizes the dominant of G, and
then reaches its climax with the return of Ex. 10, suddenly in
the key of B-flat, at measure 371. The tempo is increased at
measure 373, and Ex. 10 is treated in rising sequences, moving

from B-flat to G-flat and then to E major at measure 377, where a fragment of Ex. 10 is set contrapuntally against another fragment of the same theme:

The passage moves into G major at measure 381, where a repeated brass figure based on the intervals of Ex. 1 grows in intensity and volume.

CODA

Measures 387-407. At the climax of this crescendo, a figure drawn from Ex. 10 (see treble clef part in example above) is contrapuntally set against Ex. 1, triple forte. As Ex. 1 continues, the fragment of Ex. 10 functions as an ostinato figure in increasing rhythmic diminution, beginning at measure 391. The passage is suddenly terminated at measure 394, and Ex. 3 is heard over a low E-flat pedal point, quietly at first but gradually increasing in volume as the chromatically descending minor triads are treated in sequence. A hint of Ex. 4 appears at measure 399, still over the pedal point, and Ex. 8 is stated in fortissimo at measure 401, followed by a concluding flourish on the tonic chord.

SECOND MOVEMENT

Form	Ternary
Section A	measures 1-58
Section B	measures 59-127
Section A'	measures 128-151

SECTION A

Measures 1-24. The movement opens quietly with a slow series of minor triads in parallel motion, over which is heard a broad melody at measure 4.

Ex. 1

This theme resembles Ex. 11 of the opening movement. It is here stated first by the English horn and then, after another series of parallel chords, by full strings at measure 12. Expansion of Ex. 1 leads to a figure, beginning at measure 17, in which the interval of the fourth is stressed. The figure is imitated by various solo instruments, grows in volume and then subsides.

Measures 25-58. A quiet harmonic progression leads into a melody on solo horn, stated softly over repeated chords:

Ex. 2

The interval of the fourth is again stressed here, both in the bass movement of the harmonic progression and in the horn solo itself. The passage continues, with changed instrumentation in the melody, and a short crescendo leads to the return of Ex. 1 at measure 39, developing to a fortissimo at measure 43. The music subsides, and at measure 52 Ex. 2 is quietly stated and fades to silence on a held C major chord.

SECTION B

Measures 59-107. Solo viola introduces a new melody, answered by solo clarinet at measure 63:

Ex. 3

Example 3, which is stated briefly, leads immediately to a short figure at measure 70, stated first by solo clarinet and then by piccolo over a string tremolo:

Ex. 4

This figure is a variant of an actual London street cry.[3] It is developed into a melody in low strings, extended, and built to a climax at measure 89, where Ex. 3, suddenly pianissimo, is stated as a long, lyric melodic line. A brief crescendo and diminuendo lead to a restatement of Ex. 4 by English horn at measure 98. Again Ex. 4 is expanded, and a crescendo is built.

Measures 108-127. At the climax of this crescendo, Ex. 3 returns, forte, and through use of sequences and abrupt changes in dynamic levels, continues its expansion to a fortissimo at measure 121. A gradual diminuendo leads to a quiet, held tone in the strings.

SECTION A'

Measures 128-151. Minor triads in parallel motion introduce the return of Ex. 1 at measure 129, in shortened form. Example 2 is restated, also briefly, at measure 139, and the

movement concludes with the pianissimo statement by solo
viola, beginning at measure 145, of Ex. 3.

THIRD MOVEMENT: Scherzo (Nocturne)

Form	Scherzo and two Trios
Section A	measures 1-195 (including repeat)
Section B (Trio I)	measures 196-223
Section A'	measures 224-292
Section C (Trio II)	measures 293-362
Section A''	measures 363-419
Coda	measures 420-491

The title of this movement may appear contradictory, the
terms "scherzo" and "nocturne" usually connoting entirely
contrasting moods. However, Vaughan Williams has used
the latter term here in its most literal sense. The Scherzo is
thus meant to depict London at night.[4]

SECTION A

Measures 1-54. After a brief introduction, the main theme
of the Scherzo appears at measure 13. It takes various forms,
all of which emphasize the interval of the fourth:

Ex. 1

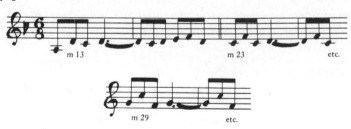

All forms of Ex. 1 bear an identical rhythmic pattern, which
renders them interchangeable in the course of the rapidly
moving and highly rhythmic passages that constitute much

of this movement. The music builds to a forte at measure 39, in which a rhythmic figure is repeated, and then subsides to the quiet restatement of Ex. 1 at measure 45. Descending sequences, followed by a rising scale passage, result in a movement from the prevailing tonic of D minor (Dorian) into B-flat minor.

Measures 55-98. A new figure appears in the low register at measure 55.

Ex. 2

A crescendo is built upon this figure, employing Ex. 2 in rising sequence and a brass chord figure involving hemiola rhythmic patterns. At measure 70, the passage subsides to a pianissimo statement of Ex. 2 in a higher register. The figure assumes the function of an ostinato, as a brief bassoon motive is heard under it at measure 72, and a solemn trombone statement beginning at measure 77. A sudden crescendo and diminuendo lead to another statement of Ex. 2 at measure 86, first heard in high winds, then bassoons, and finally subsiding on a rising violin figuration.

Measure 99-195. This is an exact repetition of measures 1-98 above, with a single exception. The bassoon statement of Ex. 2 (measure 90 above, measure 188 here) is now repeated and expanded by other instruments in the lower register, leading directly into the first Trio section.

SECTION B (TRIO I)

Measures 196-223. At a sudden fortissimo, horns and low strings appear with a descending melodic figure:

This is based upon Ex. 2 and treated in rhythmic augmentation. It is immediately imitated canonically at measure 199 and again at measure 202, subsiding on a rhythmic figure heard previously (see measures 39-44). After a short crescendo and diminuendo, the passage leads quietly into the return of the Scherzo.

SECTION A'

Measures 224-292. The music now returns from B-flat to D minor, and Ex. 1 is heard at measure 224. There is a sudden shift to the major mode (D major) at measure 257 and a gradual crescendo. The music subsides to a pianissimo statement of Ex. 2 as an ostinato, under which the bassoon figure and trombone passage reappear (see measures 72 and 77). Example 2 once more dominates the texture at measure 276, and is expanded into a descending passage for bassoon and cello. This passage leads directly into the second Trio and also serves to move from D (Aeolian) into C major.

SECTION C (TRIO II)

Measures 293-362. The orchestra imitates a harmonica, or accordion, and an extended melody is then presented by flute and oboe at measure 299. Note the change in time signature to 2/4.

Ex. 3

etc.

The lilt of the melody, its pentatonic construction, the syncopated accompaniment and the previously noted mouth-organ imitations all suggest a street tune.[5] At measure 313 the tune is repeated with fuller orchestration, and then subsides to a

figure reminiscent of Ex. 1, once more in 6/8 meter, at measure 327. This figure and Ex. 3 are combined contrapuntally
and treated in descending sequence, finally subsiding on a
string figuration that leads directly into the return of the
Scherzo.

SECTION A''

Measures 363-419. Example 1 is extended and developed
to a fortissimo at measure 381, at which point the music
moves into D major. The bassoon figure noted previously
(see measures 72-73, 267-270) is restated at measure 385,
and is then treated in rhythmic augmentation at measure 389
under a continuing ostinato of Ex. 1:

etc.

The augmentation is further increased to dotted-quarter
values, as the figure is stated fortissimo by full brass at measure 394. This passage leads directly to a fortissimo restatement of Ex. 1, beginning at measure 400, which quickly subsides to a quiet imitation, by various instrumental combinations, of a melodic fragment, and finally dies away on a held
note D.

CODA

Measures 420-491. A quiet passage for strings, in which a
chord with added lowered sixth predominates, alternates with
fragmentary statements of Ex. 1. The string passage is extended, beginning at measure 450, and Ex. 1 is heard again,

only briefly, at measure 465. A more complete statement of Ex. 1, beginning at measure 475, is extended by solo bassoon, and is treated in increasing rhythmic augmentation. The movement reaches a quiet conclusion on a held D minor chord.

FOURTH MOVEMENT

Form	Ternary
Introduction	measures 1-15
Section A	measures 16-69
Section B	measures 70-120
Section A′	measures 121-159
Coda	measures 159-173
Epilogue	measures 174-234

INTRODUCTION

Measures 1-15. The movement begins on a sharp dissonance for full orchestra, leading to a succession of parallel chords descending chromatically, and a fortissimo at measure 7. The passage subsides on a brief melodic figure, beginning at measure 10, which is repeated twice more as the music fades to a pianissimo.

Ex. 1

Ex. 2

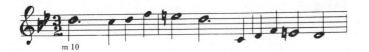

SECTION A

Measures 16-69. A slow theme is stated at measure 16, marked "Maestoso alla marcia," in the key of G. The lowered seventh degree and changing inflections of the third and sixth degree, however, impart a modal (Aeolian and Mixolydian) character to the theme.

Ex. 3

Example 3 is built in two symmetrical four-measure phrases which are immediately repeated (beginning at measure 24) with fuller orchestration and the addition of a countermelody in high strings. As the passage subsides to a pianissimo, the last phrase is again repeated, measures 32-36.

A quiet series of chromatically descending chords begins at measure 36 and alternates with fragments of Ex. 3 set in parallel chord motion for wind and brass, leading directly into a richly orchestrated statement of the second phrase of Ex. 3, beginning at measure 45. A gradual crescendo builds to a fortissimo flourish for brass on the G major chord, which quickly subsides.

The series of chromatically descending chords is resumed, pianissimo, at measure 56, and quickly grows in intensity and rhythmic movement. At measure 63 a short figure is introduced, answered by a march-like movement in the bass:

Ex. 4

Note the use of parallel chord progressions in Ex. 4, which, like those of Ex. 1, are reminiscent of Ex. 3 of the first movement. Example 4 is expanded, as the descending chord blocks and the marching bass figure are set contrapuntally against one another in rising and falling sequences. A gradual crescendo leads to a fortissimo at measure 70.

SECTION B

Measures 70-120. A new theme appears at measure 70, at the climax of the crescendo:

Ex. 5

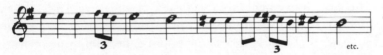

This figure is heard three times, punctuated by the rhythmic bass line of Ex. 4. Example 4 itself appears at measure 77, in an extended sequential treatment that grows from piano to fortissimo and then subsides. At measure 86, Ex. 5 returns, combined contrapuntally with Ex. 4, and another crescendo leads to a fully scored, fortissimo statement of Ex. 5 at measure 96. The passage reaches its climax at measure 103, and an extended series of descending minor triads (again reminiscent of Ex. 3, first movement), rapidly diminishing in volume, subsides at measure 110.

Example 5 suddenly appears at measure 111, fortissimo and at a slower tempo, answered by an echo of Ex. 4. The two motives alternate, and fade into a quiet statement of Ex. 2 at measure 117.

SECTION A'

Measures 121-159. Example 3 is quietly presented by strings at measure 121, and is expanded into a long crescendo. At measure 137, the chromatically descending line of

Ex. 1 is added to the texture, and at measure 147 the two motives alternate in increasing crescendo, climaxed by a triple-forte statement of Ex. 1 at measure 151. Example 1 subsides over a G pedal point and leads into a final restatement of Ex. 2 at measure 155, still over the G pedal, and a sudden crescendo at measure 159.

CODA

Measures 159-173. The music grows suddenly quiet on the G major chord plus lowered sixth of the first movement. Example 3 of that movement is heard briefly, beginning at measure 160, over an E-flat pedal point, and a fragment of Ex. 4 of the first movement also appears at measure 162. These reminders fade into the held chord (noted above at measure 159), and Big Ben is heard once more, beginning at measure 167.[6] There is a brief moment of complete silence.

EPILOGUE

Measures 174-234. A quiet ostinato figuration, built on the B-flat minor triad, appears at measure 174, and a pattern of rising fourths is introduced into the texture at measure 176. A series of sequences serves to guide the passage through various minor keys, finally resuming in G major (pentatonic) at measure 203, at which point the material of the symphony's introduction is reiterated. (See Ex. 1, first movement.) Example 2 of the finale is heard briefly, beginning at measure 212, and the dissonance that opened the last movement appears, pianissimo in brass, at measure 223. A fully-scored G major chord, beginning at measure 225, swells from a pianissimo to a forte, and then gradually dies away.

❖   ❖   ❖

In discussing this work, one must invariably deal with the fact that it bears a title and contains within it references to London street cries and the Westminster Chimes. Is it, therefore, to be classified as program music? Opinions are divided on this matter. Foss claims that "in a country where opera is not a native growth [Vaughan Williams] crammed an opera into a symphonic mold. *A London Symphony* is too picturesque to be admissible as a pure symphony, but is so living as to be lovable as a gigantic scena. . . ."[7] Ottaway adds that the material is "heterogeneous, evocative and picturesque . . . rather closer to the immediate facts of experience than the form will allow."[8] The composer himself, however, has denied the existence of a specific program, urging that "if hearers recognize a few suggestions of such things as the Westminster Chimes or the lavender cry here or there, they are asked to consider these as accidents, not essentials of the music."[9] In this respect, Vaughan Williams' comments are similar to those made by Beethoven concerning his *Pastorale* Symphony.

The solution to the dilemma may lie in the substitution of the term "impressionistic" for "program music." The influence of the French impressionists upon Vaughan Williams is apparent in the actual sound of the music. The composer notes that he unconsciously "cribbed" the Introduction from Debussy's *La Mer*.[10] Moreover, impressionism is reflected in the evocative, suggestive references to the sounds of London. In Howes's words, "if the London Symphony is not a guide book it nevertheless evokes memories of London; it portrays the spirit of the place. . . ."[11] W. R. Anderson describes the work as the product of "subjective reflection . . . rather than of objective reporting,"[12] and therefore prefers the two middle movements to the outer ones.

The music thus consists of many ideas, motives and melodic fragments, developed simultaneously or in rapid succession. The modified use of cyclic form, as in *A Sea Symphony*, serves to organize this mass of material. Finally, *A London Symphony*, in its unified presentation of widely heterogeneous elements, is very much like the city itself.

Pastoral Symphony

In his program notes for the first performance of the *Pastoral Symphony* in 1922, Vaughan Williams wrote, "the music of this symphony is almost entirely quiet and contemplative."[1] It is this quality of sustained introspection that distinguishes the *Pastoral Symphony* from its two predecessors, particularly the more objective, extroverted *A London Symphony*. Foss has noted that the city of London seems to have drawn out the peasant in the composer, while the countryside stimulated his more poetic nature.[2] Howes, attempting to relate the music to a specific landscape, concludes that the scenery is "not spectacular" and that the symphony may reflect Vaughan Williams' memories of Northern France, where he was stationed during his military service in World War I.[3]

The work is similar to its predecessors, however, in one important respect: it bears a suggestive, semiprogrammatic title, and is thus related, if only in initial inspiration, to extramusical phenomena.

FIRST MOVEMENT

Form	Sonata-Allegro
Exposition	measures 1-62
Development	measures 63-101
Recapitulation	measures 102-147
Coda	measures 148-188

EXPOSITION

Measures 1-62. A weaving pattern of triads in parallel motion is heard at the beginning of the work. This pattern

58

sets the slow pace of the entire movement (tempo "Molto
moderato") and serves as an ostinato background for the entrance of a slow melody at measure 4:

Ex. 1

The theme is pentatonic, gives a strong impression of G major
(Mixolydian), and outlines the interval of a rising fifth.

In Ex. 1 the weaving pattern persists over the theme, although the theme is accompanied by its own chord pattern.
This technique of setting parallel chord lines, rather than
single melodic lines, contrapuntally against one another is a
consistent feature of the entire symphony. Tovey, in noting
the technique in this work, comments that "two or even three
melodic threads may run simultaneously, each loaded with
its own chord, utterly regardless of how their chords collide.
. . . Bi-planar or tri-planar harmony is what the theorists
call it, and it is both more schematic and more free in this
work than in most of the examples that have been discussed
. . . during the last twenty years."[4]

At measure 9, an answering theme appears in solo violin,
imitated at measure 10 by solo oboe. This melodic figure is
also pentatonic — Mixolydian in contour.

Ex. 2

This leads to a more richly orchestrated version of Ex. 1

at measure 12, and Ex. 1 is treated expansively. At measure 25 a brief cadential figure is introduced by the entire woodwind choir over held string chords:

Ex. 3

The figure is answered by a brief motive on the English horn, beginning at measure 28, and then answered in imitation by solo clarinet and solo violin.

Ex. 4

Other solo voices, such as oboe and viola, are added to the texture. At measure 41 an extended melody is introduced by 'celli and imitated by solo clarinet at measure 45:

Ex. 5

The clarinet statement leads to another cadential figure, a brief motive harmonized with triads in parallel motion and resolving on the A major chord. (See measure 49.)

Ex. 6

Quiet chords for divided strings lead to another brief state-

ment of Ex. 6 at measure 51, followed by an extended passage
for solo oboe over a series of descending triads in muted horns
and harp. Another statement of Ex. 6 by strings and winds,
beginning at measure 59, is quietly resolved on a held A major
triad in divided strings.

DEVELOPMENT

Measures 63-90. The weaving pattern of the movement's
opening is established over the held A major chord, and Ex. 1
is added to the texture, stated by horns at measure 64. It is
taken up by trumpets, at measure 66, in imitation. The texture is abruptly lightened at measure 72, as Ex. 1 is presented
by solo violin, against a background of string tremolo, quietly
descending parallel chord series, and solo flute obligato. Solo
oboe, bassoon and clarinet variants of Ex. 1 appear, beginning
at measure 80, and a fragment of Ex. 1 is treated sequentially
by low strings and harp, beginning at measure 87. The texture is again weighty.

Measures 91-101. A gradual crescendo begins at measure
91, built upon a sequential treatment of Ex. 3. As Ex. 3 is
presented in rhythmic augmentation, the music begins to
subside at measure 95. Descending sequences and a diminuendo lead to a held chord, pianissimo, in low strings.

RECAPITULATION

Measures 102-147. Example 2 is stated by solo oboe, immediately imitated by solo flute and clarinet, at measure 104.
Example 1 is heard on solo horn at measure 106 but subsides
into a short descending melodic figure, imitated in stretto
by various orchestral combinations. The opening figure of
Ex. 1 is presented by divided strings at measure 112 and is
joined to Ex. 3, which is then repeated by solo horn over
pianissimo string chords.

Example 4 is presented by solo English horn and imitated
by solo viola and clarinet, all over a quietly moving bass line

in low strings. At measure 127 Ex. 5 begins in the violas, taken up by the entire string section and treated expansively, leading directly to a sequential melodic statement of Ex. 6. Ascending sequences lead to a forte at measure 138 and to further statements of Ex. 6 as the intensity subsides. There is a gradual diminuendo as solo instruments imitatively elaborate upon a brief melodic figure.

CODA

Measures 148-188. There is a slight increase in tempo at measure 148, and an ostinato pattern of weaving triads is established. Example 1 is presented by solo horn at measure 149, answered by high woodwinds at measure 153 and low strings at measure 155. Violins take up the melody at measure 157, and a crescendo builds to a climax at measure 162 followed by a rapid diminuendo.

Another gradual crescendo begins at measure 164, built upon Ex. 1 treated as a ground bass.

Various instrumental colors present Ex. 1 in augmentation above the ground, as the texture and intensity increase. The passage subsides to a pianissimo statement of Ex. 3 at measure 179, followed by Ex. 4 on unaccompanied solo English horn. The movement concludes with a final statement of Ex. 1, triple-piano, by muted low strings.

SECOND MOVEMENT

Form	Ternary (Song with repeated Trio)
Section A	measure 1-67
Section B	measures 67-75
Section A'	measures 75-112
Section B'	measures 112-128

There is a lack of contrast between this movement and the opening movement. Both are slow in tempo ("Molto Moderato" and "Lento Moderato" respectively), and both maintain a tranquil mood.

SECTION A

Measures 1-67. The movement begins with an extended melody, stated by solo horn over a sustained F minor chord in the strings.

Ex. 1

Example 1 is answered by a series of ascending parallel triads in the strings, leading to a brief figure based upon the end of Ex. 1 (bracketed above). Over a quiet stringed accompaniment, solo oboe and clarinet present Ex. 1, beginning at measure 14, again subsiding upon the (bracketed) concluding figure, which is echoed by solo horn.

After a brief silence, a steady eighth-note ostinato figuration is established in the strings, beginning at measure 22, and a variant of Ex. 1 is introduced by solo flute and viola. Other short melodic figures are stated by solo instruments and answered imitatively, against the steady eighth-note figuration. Another extended variant of Ex. 1, beginning at measure 38, produces a short crescendo and a forte at measure 48. Solo 'cello and oboe introduce another variant of the basic melody at measure 52, answered by a quiet passage for divided strings in which parallel triads begin to dominate the texture. An extended parallel chord series then leads to a held chord of E-flat major.

SECTION B

Measures 67-75. Against the E-flat triad, which then is

developed into a parallel chord series, a new theme is stated softly by a *natural* E-flat trumpet.

Ex. 2

etc.

The natural trumpet is expressly called for in the score "so that only natural notes may be played and that the B-flat (7th partial) and D (9th partial) should have their true intonation."[5] Howes refers to this passage as "the fanfare with the flat seventh," and relates the idea to an experience Vaughan Williams had while in military service, when he heard a camp bugler "hit the seventh as a missed shot for the octave."[6]

Much of the fanfare (beginning at measure 73) is unmeasured, played as a cadenza over a sustained E-flat major triad.

SECTION A'

Measures 75-112. Example 1, tutti and fortissimo, interrupts the solo fanfare at measure 75, quickly subsiding to a quiet statement of the concluding figure (bracketed in Ex. 1) in high strings. A variant of Ex. 1 is presented by solo clarinet at measure 86 and answered by English horn at measure 93, against a quiet eighth-note ostinato pattern. A short crescendo leads to a climax at measure 102, which subsides on a series of chords in parallel motion. These come to rest on a sustained F major triad in divided strings.

SECTION B'

Measures 112-128. Against the background of triads in divided strings, Exx. 1 and 2 are combined contrapuntally.

Example 1 is played on solo clarinet against Ex. 2 on a *natural* F horn.

The passage subsides, and an ascending parallel chord series concludes on a brief reference to the final (bracketed) figure of Ex. 1, and a held F minor triad in the first inversion for high strings.

THIRD MOVEMENT

Form	Scherzo with repeated Trio
Section A	measures 1-46
Section B (Trio)	measures 47-103
Section A'	measures 104-133
Section B' (Trio)	measures 134-157
Section A''	measures 158-171
Coda	measures 172-227

SECTION A

Measures 1-46. The main theme of the Scherzo is stated immediately by low strings and bassoon:

Ex. 1

It is answered by a brass figure, beginning at measure 11,

which continues over a rhythmic pattern in strings.

Ex. 2

Expansion of Ex. 2 leads to a crescendo, and a fortissimo statement of Ex. 1 by full orchestra at measure 20. The passage subsides to a flute melody, presented over an ostinato of tremolo strings and harp, beginning at measure 27.

Ex. 3

This is imitated by solo violin at measure 31 and is then set contrapuntally against the return of Ex. 1 at measure 35. A gradual crescendo builds to a climax at measure 47.

SECTION B (TRIO)

Measures 47-103. At measure 47, a new theme is introduced by brass, fortissimo. The melody is in the Mixolydian mode, on G:

Ex. 4

Example 4 is composed of two short phrases, forming a parallel period. The initial figure of the melody (bracketed above) is developed sequentially, beginning at measure 55, and then treated as a repeated ground bass in low strings, over which a gradual crescendo is built. Example 4 is restated in complete form, fortissimo and fully scored, at measure 74. Its expansion through the development of the (bracketed) figure, as before, builds to a fortissimo at measure 96, and a variant of Ex. 4, triple-forte, leads directly into the return of the Scherzo.

SECTION A'

Measures 104-133. Example 1 is stated, suddenly quiet, at measure 105 and is answered by Ex. 3 at measure 114, stated by solo flute and imitated by solo oboe at measure 118. Example 2 is added to the texture, stated by horns at measure 120 and immediately imitated by trombones. A sudden crescendo leads to a fortissimo statement of Ex. 1 at measure 128, and another sudden crescendo builds to a climax at measure 134.

SECTION B' (TRIO)

Measures 134-157. Example 4 is stated by full orchestra, fortissimo, at measure 134, and is developed as before, subsiding in volume and then building to a climax at measure 158.

SECTION A''

Measures 158-171. A struck cymbal introduces the restatement, fortissimo, of Ex. 1. The music rapidly diminishes in volume, and muted strings present a descending sequence built on a figure of Ex. 1. The passage concludes on a sustained note G in low (muted) strings.

CODA

Measures 172-227. Over the sustained G pedal in double-bass, a new theme is introduced by the violas, at a rapid tempo (Presto). It is imitated canonically by the other strings:

Ex. 5

At measure 180, a variant of Ex. 3 appears in counterpoint to the string passage, stated first by solo flute and then answered imitatively by solo clarinet, oboe, bassoon and horn. At measure 187, Ex. 2 is added to the texture, appearing in flutes and clarinets. Other instruments take up Ex. 2, beginning at measure 190, and the introduction of the celesta (stating Ex. 2) at measure 192 adds new color to the orchestral fabric. The passage subsides on a descending figure for strings, which reaches a sustained low E. On this E pedal, the canonic imitation of Ex. 5 begins again in the strings, beginning at measure 200. Example 2 appears at measure 202, Ex. 3 at measure 206, and the passage concludes on a sustained high G, in tremolo violins, at measure 212.

A series of descending triads is heard against the high G, leading to a statement of Ex. 1 at measure 221, at a slower tempo. Example 1, in high winds, harp and celesta, is set against a figure of Ex. 5 in low strings, and the movement concludes quietly on a G major triad.

FOURTH MOVEMENT

Form	Sonata-Allegro
Introduction	measures 1-5
Exposition	measures 5-55
Development	measures 56-109
Recapitulation	measures 110-155
Coda	measures 155-157

INTRODUCTION

Measures 1-5. This final movement, like the first two movements, is slow in tempo and relatively tranquil in mood. It opens with a wordless vocal solo (soprano or tenor)[7] over a quiet tympani roll. Like the natural trumpet solo of the second movement, the melody takes the form of an unmeasured cadenza.

Ex. 1

It subsides on a held note E at measure 5, at which point the movement proper begins.

EXPOSITION

Measures 5-55. An ascending figure is quietly presented by muted strings, and this figure develops into a more expanded melodic line at measure 14, scored for woodwinds, horns and harp.

Ex. 2

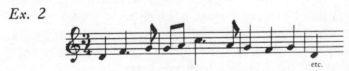

Both Exx. 1 and 2 above are pentatonic and are related in their contours to many of the themes and figures previously presented in the symphony.

A figure of Ex. 2 assumes importance when stated by solo oboe at measure 21 and is expanded into a repeated pattern (beginning at measure 24) which is contrapuntally set against Ex. 2:

Ex. 3

etc.

Low strings are added to the texture at measure 32, entering with a statement of Ex. 2, and higher strings present
Ex. 3 at measure 39. A short crescendo builds to a climax at
measure 46 and gradually subsides to a brief silence.

DEVELOPMENT

Measures 56-109. The music becomes suddenly agitated at
measure 56, characterized by extreme changes in tempo and
dynamics from measure to measure and by the use of string
tremolo. Beginning at measure 59, Ex. 1 is presented by two
solo instruments: English horn at measure 59, solo violin at
measure 67, each alternating with agitated string passages
involving tremolo, *sul tasto* and *sul ponticello* bowings.

Example 2 appears in low winds and horns at measure 72,
answered by a reference to Ex. 6 of the first movement, and
subsiding to a quiet passage for strings and harp. Solo 'cello
variants of Ex. 1 are set against a string tremolo background
and a sustained tone in solo violin, beginning at measure 78.
The 'cello melody is then answered imitatively by solo flute,
at measure 88, leading to alternating statements of Ex. 6
(first movement) in the brass and a variant of Ex. 1 in the
solo violin. A sudden crescendo leads to a fortissimo at
measure 107, in which a figure similar to Ex. 3 is repeated
with increasing intensity.

RECAPITULATION

Measures 110-155. At a slower tempo, Ex. 1 is stated by
full orchestra, triple-forte, in unison and octave doublings.

The passage quickly subsides on a descending melodic figure for strings, which then serves as an ostinato pattern for the quiet entrance of Ex. 2 in low brass at measure 118. A gradual crescendo leads to a fully orchestrated statement of Ex. 2 at measure 128 and to a further expansion of the theme, characterized by sequences and overlapping canonic imitation. A fortissimo is reached at measure 142, which subsides to a quiet statement of Ex. 3 by the brass. In a slower tempo, beginning at measure 149, muted strings repeat the ascending figure related to Ex. 2 presented earlier in the movement (see measures 5-14), which reaches a sustained high A in the violins.

CODA

Measures 155-157. Against the held high A in violins, the vocal soloist again chants wordlessly in an unmeasured passage. The melody is not an exact repetition of Ex. 1, but a variant, which employs many of the melodic figures of the entire symphony. The solo passage descends to a low E, and the violins then gradually die away on the high note A.

❖   ❖   ❖

The singular lack of contrast in this work has provoked numerous comments. Neville Cardus refers to the symphony as "a monochrome in music, with tones of no luster mingling one with the other, like the cloud, light and distance in a landscape,"[8] while Ottaway considers this the "most undemonstrative" of the composer's symphonies. He adds, however, that "paradoxically, by virtue of its insistence upon a single mood it must also be accounted the most emphatic."[9] Herbert Howells, writing of the symphony shortly after its first performance, states that "even its detractors (and they may be many) will admit its compelling sense of unity, though they may count it death to the work." [10]

The detractors were indeed many, calling attention to the

unrelieved tranquillity of the piece, and questioning its compatibility with the symphonic esthetic of drama and contrast. Ottaway's comments sum up this feeling:

Four movements, similarly meditative in mood and tempo . . . that is rather a tall order, not to mention the little audible contrast within each movement. Is it really a symphonic experience to "stand and stare," whatever the depth of one's musings? . . . Apart from the more obviously folky tunes, it is obviously a work of "sensation" music. The Impressionists made of sensation an absolute value, but they knew that their ways were unsuited to Symphony. . . . In seeking to evoke spaciousness — the timeless landscape — the composer has failed to make the Pastoral musically spacious. . . .[11]

Foss notes that another derisive critic described the symphony as "like a cow looking over a gate," and replies, "I saw that same, that universal cow, only this morning. Vaughan Williams remembered it in London, and told us about it."[12]

The *Pastoral Symphony* resembles its two predecessors in the use of such musical techniques as modal and pentatonic melodies, parallel chord progressions and extensive solo passages. These means are used, however, for effects unlike anything previously attempted by Vaughan Williams. Foss notes:

in the eight years that divide the first version of the *London* (1914) from the *Pastoral* (1922) he [Vaughan Williams] seems to have become musically a different man . . . in the earlier [symphony] the composer was addressing an audience, in the later he was talking to himself. The one dramatized external things, was objective, anthropomorphic, theatrical . . . the other was . . . impersonal, ruminative, subjective . . . From *A London Symphony* one can quote, never from the *Pastoral*.[13]

Unlike *A London Symphony,* no specific references or associations suggest that the *Pastoral Symphony* is programmatic. In both symphonies, however, the techniques of French impressionism are utilized, and in both the "program" is one of indirect association rather than direct tone-painting. Ottaway's comments notwithstanding, both works deal with "experiences" rather than "sensations," and are more closely related to Beethoven's *Symphony Pastorale* than to Debussy's *La Mer*. There are obvious differences between Vaughan Williams' and Beethoven's conceptions of the pastoral, but these may derive merely from the fact that Beethoven was (by his own admission) a visitor to the countryside and Vaughan Williams a native of it.

Symphony in F Minor, Number 4

THE SYMPHONY IN F MINOR,[1] 1935, is the first of the composer's symphonies to be designated by key and not by a programmatic title. As Howes states, "there is no specific subject . . . which it can be said to be about. Its subject is contained within it and is of a logical nature."[2]

Nevertheless, it is worth noting that analysts and critics of the symphony, by affixing labels of their own choosing to the title of the work, have assumed some programmatic implication. Howes himself refers to the symphony as the "Fascist,"[3] while Foss calls it the "Romantic."[4] Mellers, while attaching no label, claims that "the Fourth is the most obviously dramatic work that Vaughan Williams ever wrote."[5]

The title "Fascist" is singularly intriguing; it connotes a relationship between the work and the political state of Europe during and after its composition. Many critics, again, are convinced that such a relationship exists. Foss states that the "tortuous F minor relates in 1932-34 to no single incident, rather to a world-state of turmoil. . . . I do not think it fanciful to relate this stupendous work . . . to the state of the world in the early nineteen-thirties, when it was written. . . ."[6] In Ottaway's words, "it is the work of a man . . . meeting the impact of the modern world."[7] N. Gerrard Long claims that "clearly the work must be related to its period . . . in this surprising work Vaughan Williams, so often the dreamer, has expressed the reality of a distasteful world."[8]

These outspoken comments were provoked by the nature of the music itself, which is markedly different from the composer's earlier works. Technically, it is surprisingly dissonant and heavily orchestrated. Emotionally, it conveys an impression of urgency, violence and great power, a power characteristic of the growing militancy and agonizing tension of the 1930's.

Two musical ideas function as leitmotifs throughout the four movements of the work. The first of these motives (motive A below) is composed of major and minor seconds:

Motive A

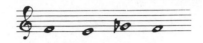

Motive B is built on an ascending pattern of fourths:[9]

Motive B

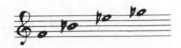

FIRST MOVEMENT

Form	Sonata-Allegro
Introduction	measures 1-48
Exposition	measures 49-122
Development	measures 123-178
Recapitulation	measures 179-240

INTRODUCTION

Measures 1-48. The work begins, fortissimo, on the dissonance of a minor ninth resolving to the octave. Sequential treatment of this pattern leads to a statement of motive A at measure 6, imitated canonically and in rhythmic diminution. Motive B is played by full brass at measure 14 and repeated in diminution by strings and winds. This entire section is repeated, beginning at measure 20, and extended through rising sequences. Motive B is presented in diminution in low brasses at measure 43, as a countersubject to the prevailing melodic sequence, and the passage reaches a climax at measure 46. A short figure is stated, fortissimo, by full orchestra in two-part canon, terminating abruptly at measure 49.

EXPOSITION

Measures 49-84. The meter changes from 6/4 to 3/2, and a rhythmic ostinato pattern is introduced at measure 49. At measure 52 a long melodic line, doubled in full strings, is stated over the ostinato.

Ex. 1

This melody resembles the opening figure of the Introduction (see measures 1-6). In both, an interval of a second is followed by a descending skip.

An extended sequential passage, based upon the conflict of rhythmic patterns between Ex. 1 and its ostinato background, builds to a climax at measure 81. Example 1 is stated slowly, fortissimo, and answered canonically.

Measures 84-122. 6/4 meter is resumed as another ostinato figure is established, a march-like bass figure, beginning at measure 84, which is a variant in inversion of motive B. An extended melodic figure is introduced over this ostinato at measure 85:

Ex. 2

This melody (Ex. 2 above) is derived from motive A in its use of major and minor seconds embellishing a repeated tone. The passage is developed sequentially, shifting from the key of D major to E-flat major at measure 95. The third scale degree is emphasized, alternating between the major and minor inflection (measures 95-106). The key of D major is resumed at measure 107, where the ostinato figure assumes greater importance and is played in augmentation by full strings. A fragment of Ex. 2 is extended in a rising sequence, and a brief crescendo leads to a fortissimo climax at measure 123.

DEVELOPMENT

Measures 123-178. The dissonant ninths of the movement's opening measures are stated, then followed by a sudden pianissimo. Over a quiet string tremolo, solo woodwinds develop a fragment of motive A (the descending minor second) into an ascending sequence. A sudden crescendo leads to a fortissimo statement of motive A, rhythmically altered, at measure 151. Another ascending sequence, built upon fragments of motive A and resembling measures 9-14, begins at measure 162. Motive B is stated at measure 170, then repeated in diminution against a figure based on motive A.

RECAPITULATION

Measures 179-213. A sudden return to the clashing ninths of the Introduction, fortissimo, leads to a variant of motive A at measure 184, stated in overlapping canonic imitation. After a brief silence, the rhythmic ostinato of Ex. 1 is heard at measure 189, once more in 3/2 meter, followed immediately by Ex. 1 itself at measure 190. A gradual crescendo leads to a broad statement of Ex. 1 at measure 207, which subsides, echoed softly by the brasses.

Measures 213-240. Example 2 appears, slowly and quietly,

at measure 213. Its march-like ostinato bass pattern, now treated in rhythmic augmentation, functions as a quiet counter-subject. The passage subsides, triple-piano, on a cadence in D-flat major at measure 228. At this point the accompanying ostinato of Ex. 2, still in augmentation, is stated alternately by strings and woodwinds. It has been altered to emphasize the third scale degree, which is alternately inflected major and minor, beginning at measure 234. The movement ends quietly on a sustained D-flat major triad.

SECOND MOVEMENT

Form	Sonata-Allegro
Exposition	measures 1-69
Development	measures 70-91
Recapitulation	measures 91-138

EXPOSITION

Measures 1-69. The slow movement begins with a brass statement of motive B, repeated in the woodwinds and then extended in a figure for flutes. This figure is then treated as a pizzicato ground bass, beginning at measure 7, and continues under a melody introduced by violins at measure 10.

Ex. 1

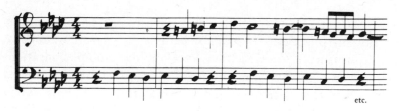

The contours of Ex. 1 and of its ground bass are similar. The melody is extended by violins and imitated canonically

at the fourth by violas and second violins, beginning at measure 17. At measure 26 a new melodic line is introduced by
solo oboe:

Ex. 2

The (bracketed) descending series of fourths in Ex. 2 are related 'to motive B. Example 2 is answered canonically, by
solo clarinet and then bassoon, finally by 'cello and double-
bass. Another melodic line is introduced at measure 38,
stated by violins and imitated canonically by violas:

Ex. 3

Example 3 is expanded and developed, with fuller orchestration, leading to an extended treatment of the descending
fourths of Ex. 2 in gradually decreasing crescendo. The intensity is heightened by repeated statements of motive B in
the brasses. The passage reaches a fortissimo at measure 56
and subsides on a pedal tone C. At measure 61, the solo
flute introduces a new melody, in C major (the dominant):

Ex. 4

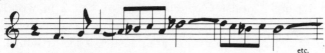

Example 4 is imitated canonically, as the C pedal (in the
double bass) begins to alternate between C and C-sharp. The
bass line descends to B at measure 70.

DEVELOPMENT

Measures 70-91. Example 2 is extended through imitation, over a pizzicato string pattern, leading to a broad passage based on Ex. 3, beginning at measure 79. Motive B appears in the brasses at measure 84 and is repeated with increasing intensity until the passage reaches a fortissimo at measure 91.

RECAPITULATION

Measures 91-138. Example 1 emerges from this fortissimo, complete with its ground bass accompaniment. The music subsides in volume as Ex. 1 is quietly presented in imitation by various solo instruments, beginning at measure 95. Example 3 is stated by solo horn at measure 108 and elaborated by full strings against a counterpoint of Ex. 2 in woodwinds (beginning at measure 116). The passage gradually resolves to a quiet cadence in F major at measure 125, at which point the solo flute again presents Ex. 4. The flute arabesque continues against a slow and quiet statement of motive A in muted trombones, and is extended into a short unmeasured cadenza, resolving quietly on a low F.

THIRD MOVEMENT

Form	Scherzo and Trio
Section A	measures 1-148
Section B (Trio)	measures 149-214
Section A′	measures 214-283
Transition to Finale	measures 284-324

SECTION A

Measures 1-101. The scherzo begins with a rapid melodic figure of ascending and descending fourths, related to motive B and in part (bracketed) reminiscent of Ex. 2, second movement:

Ex. 1

Example 1 is immediately followed by motive A, beginning at measure 5, stated in increasing diminution and finally continuing in the high registers as a rapid ostinato pattern. Under this pattern, Ex. 1, which begins again at measure 10, is developed through the sequential treatment of its characteristic (bracketed) figure. This figure is stated by various orchestral choirs, climaxed by a swirling scale passage in strings and winds (at measure 38) leading to an ostinato figuration at measure 40:

Ex. 2

At measure 48 a short melodic figure appears over this ostinato,

Ex. 3

and a more complex melodic line replaces this figure at measure 58.

Ex. 4

Example 4 is then extended through repetition, and the passage subsides to a quiet statement of motive A at measure 78, imitated in increasing diminution and followed by motive B at measure 80. At measure 85 motive A reappears in muted brass, and the antiphonal interplay between motives A and B builds to a fortissimo at measure 96, in which motive A is presented in three rhythmic values simultaneously (see below).

The most rapid of these versions of motive A is continued as a quiet ostinato pattern, subsiding to a pianissimo at measure 101.

Measures 102-148. Over the ostinato pattern of motive A, Ex. 1 appears at measure 102. It is again developed through fragmentation and sequential repetition and again builds to a swirling scale passage. At measure 133, the ostinato of Ex. 2 appears simultaneously with an extended melodic line that bears the composite characteristics of Exx. 3 and 4.

Ex. 5

This passage builds to a climax at measure 142 and then

quickly dies away, while a figure of Ex. 2 continues for a few more measures, pianissimo.

SECTION B (TRIO)

Measures 149-214. The meter changes from 6/8 to 3/4, and a melody, related to motive B in its use of fourths, is stated by tuba, bassoon and contrabassoon:

Ex. 6

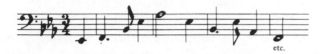

Example 6 is answered fugally, i.e. at the fifth, by trombones at measure 156, and the texture becomes more weighty with additional entrances in trumpets and clarinets. Flutes and piccolo take up the theme at measure 174 against a quiet accompaniment, and a contrapuntal treatment of Ex. 6 is resumed at measure 186, solo winds entering in canonic imitation. As the brasses take up the theme, beginning at measure 196, the texture is increased with scale passages in winds and strings, and a gradual crescendo is built, resulting in a fortissimo climax at measure 214.

SECTION A'

Measures 215-283. The return of the Scherzo is marked by a statement of Ex. 1, followed by motive A in increasing diminution and then by an extended treatment of Ex. 1 over an ostinato pattern related to motive A, which is an almost literal restatement of the movement's opening measures. As before, the expanded treatment of Ex. 1 builds to a climax of scale figurations, followed by simultaneous statements of Exx. 2 and 5 at measure 254. The passage increases in intensity as motive A (on trombones) is added to the texture at measure 268, followed by a fortissimo stretto built on Ex. 6.

The music comes to a sharp climax at measure 280 and then rapidly subsides.

TRANSITION TO FINALE

Measures 284-324. The ostinato figure of Ex. 2, now melodically built on only two notes, persists very quietly under statements of motive B, beginning at measure 288, played in turn by various solo instruments. The ninth-dissonances of the symphony's opening bars appear at measure 308 and lead (as in the first movement) to motive A at measure 316. Motive A, heard over the continued ostinato, is stated in increasing diminution, and a gradual crescendo leads directly and without pause into the finale.

FOURTH MOVEMENT (with Fugal Epilogue)

Form	Sonata-Allegro
Exposition	measures 1-114
Development	measures 115-214
Recapitulation	measures 214-308
Epilogue	measures 309-464

EXPOSITION

Measures 1-76. The movement begins, fortissimo, with a descending melodic line derived from the flute solo (Ex. 4) of the slow movement:

Ex. 1

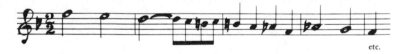

etc.

An ostinato "oom-pah" bass follows at measure 5, leading to another statement of Ex. 1 in two-voice canon. The "oom-pah" returns at measure 20, and a theme is introduced above it at measure 24. At first a simple figure, emphasizing the minor second of motive A, the theme expands to a four-measure phrase, beginning at measure 38, which is continually repeated.

Ex. 2

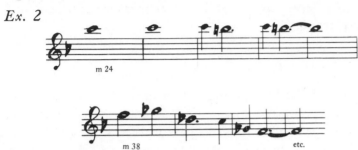

Example 2, even in its more developed form, emphasizes the minor second. In its descending skips, it also resembles Ex. 1 of the opening movement. The short phrase is repeated against the "oom-pah" background and builds to another fortissimo statement of Ex. 1, again in two-voice canon, at measure 52. The eighth-note figure of Ex. 1 is developed into an ostinato pattern, against which Ex. 2 appears in the brass at measure 62. The alternately major-minor inflection of Ex. 1 is treated antiphonally, building to a climax and then quickly subsiding at measure 74.

Measures 77-114. The marching movement of the brasses carries the key center from F downwards to B-flat major, and a martial theme is introduced at measure 77.

Ex. 3

Example 3 is related to motive B in its use of fourths, and the sequential treatment of descending fourths is reminiscent of Ex. 2 of the slow movement as well as of Ex. 1 of the

Scherzo. The asymmetrical five-measure phrase is repeated, at measure 82, and is then treated in an extensive four-voice stretto at measure 87. At measure 94, a fragment of Ex. 3 (the series of descending fourths) is treated antiphonally, leading to a brass variant of Ex. 3 at measure 106 and to a sharp crescendo.

DEVELOPMENT

Measures 115-176. Example 1 is heard at measure 115, now in the key of A major-minor. The theme is developed into a scale passage with syncopated accents. Under these, motive B appears in augmentation at measure 127, stated in the low brass. At measure 135 the "oom-pah" ostinato appears, alternating with a fragment of Ex. 2 in descending sequences and eventually subsiding to a quiet passage for muted strings against the pianissimo "oom-pah," beginning at measure 156. As "oom-pah" dies away, Ex. 2 (in its more developed form) is stated quietly by muted strings at measure 169, subsiding to silence.

Measures 177-214. A slow passage, for muted divided strings, quietly begins at measure 177. Built upon a ground bass inversion of motive B, the upper melodic line and its treatment are derived from a similar statement of Ex. 2, first movement, at the close of that movement. The passage leads to a quiet statement of motive A at measure 189, followed by motive B over a tympani pedal point. The two motives continue in alternation, and a gradual crescendo leads to an emphasized statement of motive A and a climax at measure 214.

RECAPITULATION

Measures 214-308. Example 1 is stated, fortissimo, by full orchestra and repeated twice, leading to Ex. 2 (in its initial form) at measure 223, heard against the "oom-pah" ostinato. Repetition of the initial figure of Ex. 2 leads to its more complex form at measure 237, and a sudden crescendo builds to a vigorous statement of Ex. 3 at measure 246. Example 3 appears in D major at first but is forced upwards to F major through a sequential series of canonic imitations at the fifth. A variant of Ex. 3 is stated, in F major, at measure 266, leading directly to an extended passage based upon the eighth-note figure of Ex. 1 and related to measures 116-135. As before, the accents are markedly syncopated. A variant of Ex. 2 is heard against this pattern, stated in the brass beginning at measure 285. The passage builds to a fortissimo climax at measure 302, in which F major and F minor are alternately and antiphonally stated, high orchestral forces against those in the lower registers. The alternation is interrupted by the appearance of motive A in augmentation, stated fortissimo on the trombones at measure 309.

EPILOGUE

Measures 309-464. The fugal Epilogue begins with the trombone statement of motive A, followed by reference to motive B, suddenly pianissimo in tremolo strings and woodwinds. Motive A appears once more in trombones at measure 315 and is answered at the fifth by trumpets (measure 317). The third entrance occurs at measure 323, and the texture rapidly becomes thickly contrapuntal. Motive A is presented in augmentation and diminution in this overlapping stretto, and motive B is added to the texture at measure 335. Against this polyphonic texture, composed primarily of motives A and B, other important themes of the movement appear, some of them briefly and others in more extended passages. Example 2, fourth movement, is heard at measure 354 in an extended treatment, which subsides to a pianissimo. Example 3, fourth movement, is then stated, suddenly forte, against motive A in augmentation, and is itself treated canonically. A gradual crescendo leads to a climax at measure 428, and Ex. 1, fourth movement, appears at measure 433, set against motive A in augmentation. Another gradual crescendo is climaxed by a rapid scale passage, beginning at measure 448 and ascending to a fortissimo restatement of the symphony's opening ninth-dissonances at measure 453. Ascending chords in parallel motion lead to a last statement of motive B, heard in the brass at measure 460, and six repeated ninth-dissonances. Their resolution is a single F chord, triple-forte in intensity. The third has been omitted, and the major-minor conflict is thus never resolved.

❖   ❖   ❖

The listener familiar with the earlier works of Vaughan Williams who first hears this symphony will be amazed at its striking dissonance. The work reveals, as does the *Pastoral Symphony,* one significant aspect of the composer's method: his honesty in the development of his materials, uncompromising even when the results may be unpleasant. There is no doubt that the composer was, in this instance, governed by his materials — not enslaved by them, but constantly working within the limits and implications of his original statement. The composer's own comments regarding the work are indicative of this uncompromising attitude. In a letter to Holst (1933), Vaughan Williams wrote of the symphony: "The 'nice' tunes in the Finale have already been replaced by better ones (at all event they are *real* ones). What I mean is that I *knew* the others were made-up stuff and these are not."[10] David Ewen reports Vaughan Williams as saying, with regard to the symphony, "I wrote as I felt. . . . I don't even know if I like it, but that is what I meant when I wrote it."[11] Finally, the composer commented to an orchestra, after conducting a rehearsal of the work, "Well, gentlemen, if that's modern music you can have it!"

Symphony in D Major, Number 5

WHEN THE SYMPHONY IN D MAJOR was first performed in 1943, it was instantly acclaimed by the listening public. Its success resulted from many factors, most notably the serenity of the work itself as contrasted with the severity of the war then in progress, as well as the allusions to *The Pilgrim's Progress* of John Bunyan.

Foss, in succinctly enumerating these factors, states that

Public appreciation of the D major was more immediate than that of perhaps any other single work by the composer. The circumstances of time and place can be partly discounted — the fact of the composer's age, the availability of music through radio, the contrast of the music's peace with the noise of war. Of these circumstances perhaps the most interesting was the temper of unity among the English peoples which war had induced. "Britain," writes Mr. Winston Churchill of June 1940, "was united as never before. . . ."[1]

Foss also notes that the manuscript score contains two inscriptions not reproduced on the printed score. A note on the opening page stated: "some of the themes of this Symphony are taken from an unfinished opera, 'The Pilgrim's Progress.'" Secondly, the slow movement bore an introductory quotation from the Bunyan work itself: "Upon this place stood a cross, and a little below a sepulchre. Then he said: 'He hath given me rest by his sorrow, and life by his death.'" It is also worth noting that the symphony is "dedicated without permission to Jean Sibelius."

89

FIRST MOVEMENT (Preludio)

Form   Sonatine (enlarged)[2]
Exposition   measures 1-91
Transition   measures 92-163
Recapitulation   measures 164-237

EXPOSITION

Measures 1-59. The movement opens at a moderate tempo. Over a pedal point C in low strings, a horn call is heard, introducing a rhythmic pattern that remains throughout most of the movement:

Ex. 1

The horn call is immediately answered by a figure for strings. Stated first by violins at measure 3, it is repeated with melodic decorations at measure 6 and then subsides into a restatement of the horn call. The melodic contour is pentatonic.

Ex. 2

At measure 12 a new figure is introduced in the violins, imitated in stretto by violas and 'celli. Like Ex. 2, it is pentatonic.

Ex. 3

Example 3 is expanded by full strings and winds and subsides to a pianissimo at measure 20. Example 1 is heard, again in muted horns, at measure 21, and is answered by Ex. 2 at measure 23, leading directly to a restatement of Ex. 3 at measure 33. The passage abruptly moves into the area of F minor, still over the low C pedal, at measure 40, and then settles in C minor at measure 46, as Ex. 3 is expanded over the C pedal and the persistent rhythmic pattern of Ex. 1.

Measures 60-91. There is a sudden shift into E major at measure 60 and a brightening of orchestral color as the trumpets are added to the horn figure of Ex. 1. A broad melody appears in full strings, at measure 60, against the rhythmic pattern of Ex. 1:

Ex. 4

Example 4 is expanded by full orchestra in E major, although the third, sixth and seventh degrees are occasionally lowered, implying the Aeolian mode. The passage builds in intensity, through descending sequences, measures 69-77, and then subsides to a cadential figure based upon Ex. 3. At measure 80, a short two-note figure is introduced:

Ex. 5

The minor second of Ex. 5 is again repeated at measure 86, and the E-flat is sustained against a bassoon statement of Ex. 1 in C minor. Melodic decoration of the E-flat in eighth-note string figurations leads to a rapid accelerando.

TRANSITION

Measures 92-128. At a tempo of Allegro, the eighth-note string passage continues, pianissimo, outlining the pentatonic C scale. Example 5 appears over this background, at first in unison woodwinds at measures 97 and 102, and then in contrapuntal imitation beginning at measure 104. At measure 118, the passage shifts into the area of E-flat minor, although the material and texture remain unchanged. Another contrapuntal treatment of Ex. 5 appears at measure 120, over the sustained string ostinato figurations.

Measures 129-163. There is another abrupt shift to the area of F-sharp minor, and a new motive is added to the prevailing texture. Stated by woodwinds at measure 129, it is heard against the continued string ostinato and intermittent references to Ex. 5.

Ex. 6

Example 6 above is repeated in increasing crescendo, and the tonal center shifts to F at measure 138 as the intensity continues to mount. Ascending sequences of Ex. 5 build to a triple forte at measure 147, followed by sharp statements of Ex. 6 in close stretto imitation for winds and brass. The passage gradually dies away to a quiet statement of Ex. 5 in violins at measure 158, and a gradual slowing of tempo.

RECAPITULATION

Measures 164-237. The initial tempo is resumed, and the C pedal point is again established, at measure 164. Example 1 follows immediately, and Ex. 2 is added to the texture at measure 167. A gradual crescendo leads to the return of Ex. 3, forte, at measure 179, as trombones are added to the

orchestral color for the first time in the work. Another crescendo builds to a fortissimo statement, for full orchestra, of
Ex. 4 at measure 185.

Example 4, although stated initially in B-flat major, comes to
a strong modal cadence[3] in G. The passage begins to subside
at measure 203, as Ex. 3 is softly stated by brass and answered
by Ex. 5 in low woodwinds. Example 5 is elaborated contrapuntally by woodwinds, beginning at measure 209, against a
pianissimo in low strings based on Ex. 3. A broad statement
of Ex. 6 in strings subsides upon the low C pedal point, above
which Ex. 1 appears at measure 224. The horn call (Ex. 1)
in D and a fragment of Ex. 3 in F minor alternate very
briefly. The horn call is heard last, muted and pianissimo,
over the pedal point C.

SECOND MOVEMENT

Form	Scherzo with two Trios
Section A	measures 1-183
Section B (Trio I)	measures 184-292
Section A′	measures 293-346
Section C (Trio II)	measures 347-423
Section A′′	measures 423-476

SECTION A

Measures 1-97. A rapid series of rising fourths, opening
the movement, develops into a melodic figure (bracketed below) :

Ex. 1

etc.

The ascending fourths are played in increasing rhythmic diminution. The passage is stated at first by unison strings and then in two-voice canon beginning at measure 22. Over the ostinato background of Ex. 1, a melodic figure is introduced by flutes and bassoons at measure 32.

Ex. 2

Example 2 is expanded with changed instrumentation, and a brief crescendo leads to a series of forte scale passages, beginning at measure 59, strings alternating with winds. The music subsides to a canonic statement of Ex. 1 in low woodwinds at measure 65, answered by Ex. 2 in high winds at measure 75. Strings take up Ex. 2 at measure 81 against wind figuration, and the passage is expanded through descending sequences of a fragment of Ex. 2.

Measures 98-183. A melodic figure is introduced by solo oboe and English horn at measure 98:

Ex. 3

The minor second of Ex. 3 is reminiscent of Ex. 5, first movement. Like the latter, it serves as an intrusion upon an otherwise diatonically oriented passage. Howes, referring to Ex. 3, states that "Bunyan's 'hobgoblin and foul fiend' are plainly on the prowl. . . ."[4] Example 3 alternates with a light figure in strings and flute, reminiscent of Ex. 2, and a hemiola pattern in low pizzicato strings and low woodwinds. The variant of Ex. 2 begins to dominate the texture at measure 125:

Ex. 4

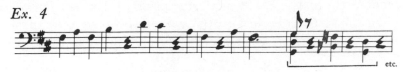

It is stated here by bassoons and low pizzicato strings and then treated by full strings and winds at measure 132. Example 3 appears in solo oboe and horn at measure 145, and the hemiola pattern (bracketed above in Ex. 4) is stated alternately by brass and winds against an ostinato scale figuration in divided strings. Example 1 is added to the texture at measure 174, stated by trombones in augmentation.

SECTION B (TRIO I)

Measures 184-292. Against the rushing string ostinato, a woodwind figure appears at measure 188, answered by the hemiola brass punctuation. After a fragment of Ex. 1 in augmentation on trombones, the short woodwind figure appears again at measure 200, again answered by the hemiola brass figure, which builds to a forte and rapidly diminishes. The figure appears in the low brasses at measure 214, now fully harmonized and set against tremolo strings (see Ex. 5 below):

Ex. 5

Example 5 is continually repeated, alternating with the hemiola figure and rushing string passages. It appears in high winds at measure 233 and then in low brasses again at measure 251, always set against the string figurations and the hemiola chord figure. A final statement of Ex. 6 by winds at measure 268 is echoed softly, without ostinato accompaniment, by low brass at measure 283, and subsides to a sustained chord.

SECTION A'

Measures 293-346. Against a sustained horn tone, Ex. 1 is heard in low strings at measure 293, and the texture increases with canonic entrances of violas, second violins and first violins at measures 301, 303 and 307 respectively. Low winds also take up Ex. 1 at measure 314, and the passage leads directly to the return of Ex. 2 at measure 325, in flute and piccolo against a rushing string ostinato. A gradual crescendo builds to a climax at measure 345 and to a sharp statement of Ex. 3 (the initial minor second) on trumpets and trombones.

SECTION C (TRIO II)

Measures 347-423. At a change in metric signature from 3/4 to 2/4, a brief figure is stated by woodwinds, beginning at measure 347. '

Ex. 6

The resemblance Ex. 6 bears to Ex. 3 is heightened by the fact that the new figure is introduced by, and then interrupted by, Ex. 3 in brasses. After its initial statement, Ex. 6 is repeated by woodwinds and then taken up by strings at measure 358. The theme is treated antiphonally, passing from winds to brasses, beginning at measure 363, and set against a reference to Ex. 1 in strings (and in 3/4 meter). The passage builds to a fortissimo statement of Ex. 6 in strings at measure 392, answered by winds and brasses. Another rapid crescendo leads to a unison statement of Ex. 6 by full orchestra at measure 410, which subsides to a pianissimo.

SECTION A''

Measures 423-476. The eighth-note figurations of Ex. 6 gradually die away, over the return of Ex. 1 in low strings and in rhythmic augmentation (due to a change of meter to 3/2). At this slower pace, Ex. 1 is expanded into a quiet passage for strings, beginning at measure 426. There is a return to the more rapid 3/4 at measure 442, and the solo bassoon enters at measure 443 with Ex. 1, answered by solo flute and finally by muted strings which rapidly descend to a low pizzicato A.

THIRD MOVEMENT (Romanza)

Form	Sonata-Allegro
Exposition	measures 1-93
Development	measures 94-147
Recapitulation	measures 148-202

EXPOSITION

Measures 1-38. At the opening of the movement, a pattern of triads is stated, pianissimo, by divided strings.

Ex. 1

The pattern of Ex. 1 serves as accompaniment for a melody on English horn, introduced at measure 7:

Ex. 2

This lyric theme, in A major (modal), leads to a broad passage for divided strings which emphasizes the interval of the fourth:

Ex. 3

The Aeolian mode is definitely established in Ex. 3, beginning at measure 12, whereas Exx. 1 and 2 are characterized by alternately raised and lowered second, third, sixth and seventh scale degrees. Example 3 is treated expansively in a contrapuntal passage that subsides to a rhythmic variant of Ex. 1 at measure 29. At measure 32 a variant of Ex. 3 is presented by solo flute:

Ex. 4

This melody is imitated canonically by other solo woodwinds, over a quiet series of parallel triads in strings, related to Ex. 1.

Measures 39-93. Example 1 appears in winds and horn, pianissimo, at measure 39, and Ex. 2 enters above it at measure 43, stated in unison strings against the woodwind pattern.

The key center of E (the dominant) is established, and the passage leads directly to an extended contrapuntal treatment of Ex. 3 for winds and divided strings, beginning at measure 47. A short crescendo leads to a forte at measure 52, and the music reaches another climax at measure 61, subsiding gradually to the rhythmic variant of Ex. 1 stated previously (see measure 29). Example 4 is stated by solo oboe at measure 72, imitated contrapuntally by English horn against the quiet background of low woodwinds. The two solo instruments then continue unaccompanied, beginning at measure 82, in a canonic variant of Ex. 4. Other woodwinds are added to the texture at measure 88, flutes and bassoons presenting a variant of Ex. 1. The quiet passage subsides into a short silence.

DEVELOPMENT

Measures 94-147. At a faster tempo, Ex. 1 is stated by strings in new rhythmic form, and a melodic figure is presented, fortissimo, by solo oboe and English horn:

Ex. 5

Example 5 is composed of elements of both Exx. 2 and 4. It is developed here in an agitated passage, involving sudden shifts of dynamics and string tremolo. The passage builds to a fortissimo at measure 112 and subsides to a quiet statement of Ex. 2 in solo horn over a string tremolo background. The horn passage is imitated by solo trumpet at the octave, beginning at measure 121, and a fortissimo passage for brass based upon a fragment of Ex. 2 leads to a climax at measure 130, in which Ex. 4 is stated in close stretto by woodwinds and strings. This activity suddenly subsides to a quiet statement of Ex. 1 at measure 135, over which a variant of Ex. 5 is presented, forte, by unison strings:

This melodic figure, in its descending minor second and minor third, resembles Ex. 5, first movement, and Exx. 3 and 6, second movement. After another quiet reference to Ex. 1, it is stated again at measure 144, building to a fortissimo two-voice canon, and subsides to a pianissimo at measure 148.

RECAPITULATION

Measures 148-202. Example 3 is presented by full strings and low winds, in A (Aeolian), as the music gradually increases in volume. High winds and brass are added to the contrapuntal texture by measure 160, and a fortissimo climax is reached at measure 166, gradually subsiding to a solo violin statement of Ex. 4, beginning at measure 178. The violin passage is interrupted by a short reference to Ex. 1 and a fragment of Ex. 2 and then dissolves into a pianissimo restatement of Ex. 1 in divided high strings. Muted solo horn presents Ex. 2 over this background at measure 191, and divided muted strings bring the movement to a close on a sustained A major triad.

FOURTH MOVEMENT (Passacaglia)

Form	Variation on a ground bass in three large sections
Section A	measures 1-67
Section B	measures 68-152
Section C	measures 153-215
Coda	measures 216-281

SECTION A

Measures 1-67. The ground bass is initially presented by
'celli, and is seven measures in length:

Ex. 1

An extended melody enters above Ex. 1 at measure 8.
Throughout much of the movement this melody serves as a
complement, or "countersubject," to Ex. 1.

Ex. 2

Howes has noted that the bracketed figure in Ex. 2 above is
reminiscent of the "Alleluia" of the Eastern Hymn "Lasst
Uns Erfreuen."[5] Against rising woodwind figurations, Ex. 2
is stated by violas, and a climax is reached at measure 34,
rapidly subsiding to a quiet passage in which Exs. 1 and 2
are treated in syncopation, A gradual crescendo, in which a
fragment of Ex. 2 is sequentially expanded over the rhythmically altered Ex. 1, leads to a fortissimo at measure 62.

SECTION B

Measures 68-152. After the ten statements of the ground
bass (Ex. 1) noted above, the variations are abruptly interrupted at measure 68[6] by a passage for brass at a faster
tempo:

This martial figure is a variant of Ex. 2, and is imitated in stretto throughout the orchestra. The passage subsides to a statement of Ex. 1 in winds and brass against pizzicato strings, beginning at measure 91. A gradual crescendo, involving contrapuntal expansion of a fragment of Ex. 1 in descending sequence, builds to a fortissimo at measure 114 in which fragments of Ex. 1 and Ex. 2 are treated in stretto against tremolo strings. The passage builds to a great climax, ending on a fortissimo D major chord for brass.

SECTION C

Measures 153-215. At measure 153 the metric signature changes from 3/4 to 4/4, and a new set of variations begins. The solo clarinet quietly presents a melodic figure against tremolo strings:

Ex. 3

This figure (Ex. 3 above) is a variant of the original ground bass (Ex. 1). Its initial clarinet statement is answered by other solo woodwinds, including a bassoon variant of Ex. 2 at measure 162.

Ex. 4

The triplet figurations (in Ex. 4 above) become more prominent from this point on through the remainder of the movement. Examples 3 and 4, like their counterparts Exx. 1 and 2, are developed simultaneously, building to a climax at measure 185 in which Ex. 3 is stated canonically by brass. This subsides momentarily but reappears at measure 194, and another contrapuntal expansion of Exx. 3 and 4 leads to a tutti climax at measure 207 in which Ex. 3 is stated in unison and octave doublings. The intensity diminishes rapidly, on a descending sequential treatment of Ex. 3, leading to another sudden crescendo and a tempo retard.

CODA

Measures 216-281. At the initial tempo of the symphony, the work's opening horn call (Ex. 1, first movement) appears at measure 216. It is heard in counterpoint with Ex. 3, which substitutes for the original C pedal point (see below).

A climax is reached at measure 221, and the passage subsides on a reference to Ex. 3, first movement, at measure 227. Example 3 is heard once more, pianissimo in low strings over the horn call, at measure 231, and leads to a quiet fragment of Ex. 2, first movement in strings. Example 2 (finale) returns quietly in divided strings at measure 236. Woodwinds are added to the texture at measure 246, as Exx. 1, 2 and 3 are in constant imitation. A low D pedal is established at measure 267, and the passage subsides on a pianissimo D major triad.

❖   ❖   ❖

It is interesting to note that commentators on this work have indulged in superlatives usually reserved only for acknowledged classic masterpieces. This high acclaim, in some instances almost approaching reverence, is rare in twentieth century criticism and is not extended to the rest of the major works of Vaughan Williams. For example, Norman Demuth states that "the Fifth Symphony . . . is out of place in a garish concert hall . . . infinitely preferable in private [rather than] communal listening . . . too intrinsically beautiful for the usual listening situations and conditions."[7] Similarly, Foss says that "the noise of clapping at the end of this Symphony is a vulgar intrusion upon the soul."[8] Howes claims that the work is "the most successful attempt since Beethoven to use music as a direct penetration of the mystery of life. . . . It is perhaps a more successful attempt than Beethoven's to deal with metaphysical issues in the language of sound."[9] And finally, Neville Cardus writes, "the Fifth Symphony contains the most benedictory and consoling music of our time."[10]

Perhaps the tensions of wartime lead men to react more strongly to art than they might otherwise do. It will be recalled, for example, that patriotic fervor in the United States during this same period resulted in similar enthusiasm for the Shostakovitch *Leningrad Symphony,* as well as in a rediscovery of the Beethoven Fifth Symphony by the general public, which was attracted by its dot-dot-dash ("V for Victory") rhythmic motif. In passing, then, one can assume that the same factors which led to the immediate success of Vaughan Williams' Fifth Symphony with the listening public affected professional musicians and critics as well. The unusual nature of the piece itself, however, must be included as one of these factors.

Of the more strictly musical matters to be considered, the relationship between the symphony and the later opera, *The Pilgrim's Progress,* is important. Many of the themes of the symphony also appear in the stage work. In an essay comparing the two works, Ottaway rejects the notion that the symphony is in any way operatic, much less programmatic. Rather, he sees the opera as a "pictorial commentary" upon the symphony.[11]

The choice of D major as the tonality of the work is also worth noting. At least one critic has commented upon the choice. In Young's words, D major is "of all classical keys the one most susceptible to interpretation through association: the key of ceremonial on the one hand and of pastoral sensibility on the other. . . ."[12] There is some indication that Vaughan Williams may have had similar reactions, for he noted that

It is admittedly harder to write good music which is joyful than that which is sad. . . . To my mind, two composers . . . have been able to write music which is at the same time serious, profound, and cheerful — Bach in the "Cum Sancto" of the B minor Mass and Beethoven in the finale of the Choral Symphony. Incidentally, both these movements are in D major.[13]

Symphony in E Minor, Number 6

LIKE THE SYMPHONY IN F. MINOR, the Symphony in E Minor, Number 6, has provoked much discussion regarding its possible extramusical implications. Howes writes that he once publicly mentioned the work, which was completed in 1948, as the "War" symphony and was sharply reproved by the composer for this.[1] Herbert Howells speaks of the symphony in terms of "apocalyptic terror,"[2] while Demuth relates it to an unsettled world.[3]

These and similar interpretations represent individual reactions to a work of high emotional impact. That reactions to this symphony are strong is understandable. It is certainly unthinkable that the composer should have devised such disturbing sounds and *not* expected people to be disturbed by them. Such a work, however, is not necessarily a literal or programmatic one, particularly if the composer himself disavows any such implications. One must agree with Hubert Foss, who, in discussing the "flood of explanatory prose which this symphony has unloosed," states that

few works of this century have occasioned a greater torrent of poppycock . . . in this music there is something that writers cannot explain, even if they understand it. In truth, no explanation is possible. Essentially this symphony speaks for itself.[4]

FIRST MOVEMENT

Form	Sonatine
Exposition:	
Subject I	measures 1-42
Bridge (development)	measures 43-82
Subject II	measures 82-129
Recapitulation	measures 129-193

Alternative interpretations have been given above for measures 43-82. Howes considers this the misplaced "development" section of the movement,[5] and cites it as an example of one musical idea creating another one through an organic growth process. The basic unity of material in the movement makes Howes's contention a reasonable and possible one. The section is listed here, however, as a conventional bridge between first and second subjects, because this seems to be a more accurate functional description.

EXPOSITION

Measures 1-42. The movement seemingly begins in F minor, and then plunges sharply into E minor:

Ex. 1

The passage continues to descend rapidly and then suddenly ascends to a repetition of Ex. 1 at measure 6. The entire process is repeated, and Ex. 1 begins again at measure 10, only to remain in the higher registers as an ostinato pattern of sixteenth notes. At measure 12, a heavy brass figure enters under this pattern and by measure 18 has developed into a series of descending minor thirds:

Ex. 2

Both Ex. 2 above and the initial brass figure at measure 12 are harmonized with minor triads in parallel motion. An extended theme appears at measure 20, stated by high strings and winds against the rapid ostinato in the lower registers.

Ex. 3

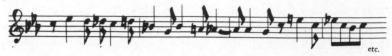

etc.

Example 3 also outlines falling thirds, alternately major and minor, and emphasizes the interval of the semitone (minor second). At measure 27 the instrumentation is reversed: the melody moves into the lower register and the ostinato to the higher. The passage builds to a loud climax at measure 33, and the downward-upward rushing of Ex. 1 continues, first in winds and then in divided strings, over a sustained tympani roll. At measure 40 there is a brief reference to Ex. 3 in low strings, which subsides to a pianissimo.

Measures 43-82. The tempo quickens, and a marching bass in 12/8 meter is established by low strings, winds and snare drum. At measure 47 a motive is introduced by trumpets and high winds, in 4/4, over the marching bass:

The motive is expanded with changed instrumentation, as it is taken up by high winds against pizzicato strings at measure 54, answered by a figure in descending minor thirds at measure 57. The martial motive and its answer are then repeated, at measure 62, and a sudden crescendo leads to a string statement at measure 72 of the descending-third figure against the 12/8 "oom-pah" bass.

etc.

The motive bears a strong resemblance to Ex. 2. There is a gradual crescendo, leading to a fortissimo at measure 79 in which the entire orchestra takes up the marching ostinato bass. This rapidly subsides to a quiet reference to the "oom-pah" bass in low strings and bassoons.

Measures 82-129. Stated by high winds and violins over a subdued version of the marching bass, a new melody appears at measure 82:

Ex. 4

In its alternation of major and minor thirds, this theme resembles Ex. 3. The outlined augmented fourth (bracketed) assumes great importance in succeeding movements. Example 4 is a broad melody, and its initial statement extends to measure 96, at which point the "oom-pah" marching bass again assumes importance. Fragments of the bridge material are repeated and extended, building to a fortissimo restatement of Ex. 4 at measure 116, presented by unison brass against the marching ostinato in full orchestra. A descending sequence based upon a fragment of Ex. 4 begins at measure 126 and comes to an abrupt halt at measure 129.

RECAPITULATION

Measures 129-159. There is a reduction in tempo and a return to the initial 4/4 meter which began the movement. The rapid figurations of Ex. 1 are heard at measure 130, quietly in the low string register, answered by high winds and full brass chords which lead to Ex. 2 at measure 144. Example 3 appears against the sixteenth-note ostinato at measure 146, fortissimo, but begins to diminish in intensity at

measure 152. The passage subsides to a quiet fragment of
Ex. 4 in low winds and horns over pianissimo trombone
chords. The fragment of Ex. 4 dies away.

Measures 160-193. At a slower tempo, and in 6/4 meter,
Ex. 4 is presented by unison strings over harp and brass
chords:

The instrumentation is expanded to a tutti, and this version
of Ex. 4 is greatly expanded, building to a climax. Its final
cadence,however, is broken by a discord at measure 188 and
the reappearance of Ex. 1 (complete, with the introductory
three notes implying F minor) in rhythmic augmentation, ending on a tutti unison E, fortissimo. The held E slowly dies
away, and leads without pause into the next movement in
B-flat, thus creating the interval of the augmented fourth.

SECOND MOVEMENT

Form	Ternary
Section A	measures 1-27
Section B	measures 28-86
Section A'	measures 86-130
Coda	measures 130-142

SECTION A

Measures 1-27. Over a held B-flat in the trumpets, a rhythmic theme is stated by unison strings and woodwinds:

Ex. 1

Example 1 contains many features presented in the opening movement, particularly the spanning of thirds through steps of semitones. It bears a distinctive rhythmic pattern, however, which is developed further in the movement. The theme is taken up by trumpets and trombones at measure 5 and then by high woodwinds against pizzicato strings at measure 11. A gradual crescendo begins as Ex. 1 is presented in unison strings over a weaving eighth-note pattern in winds, leading to a variant of Ex. 1 at measure 20 for unison strings and winds. The rhythmic pattern of Ex. 1 is presented as a descending chromatic scale, and the crescendo builds to a fortissimo at measure 24 in which the rhythmic pattern is stated in a series of augmented fourths:

At the height of its intensity, the passage is interrupted by a pianissimo tympani roll at measure 27.

SECTION B

Measures 28-86. A sudden crescendo on tympani leads to a brief figure at measure 28, stated fortissimo by full brass and tympani.

Ex. 2

Example 2 rapidly subsides to a pianissimo at measure 31, and a more expansive melody is heard softly in unison strings:

Ex. 3

etc.

Both Exx. 2 and 3 emphasize the interval of the third, and in Ex. 3 this interval is approached through semitone steps. Examples 2 and 3 are stated alternately, with changed instrumentation and dynamics, five times. On the third repetition, for pianissimo divided strings at measure 47, Ex. 2 begins to take on the chromatic characteristics of Ex. 3 and is expanded in descending semitones. Examples 2 and 3 are briefly combined contrapuntally, beginning at measure 72, and the passage subsides to a final statement of Ex. 2 in strings. This pianissimo statement evolves into a series of parallel chords, melodically emphasizing the descending third.

SECTION A'

Measures 86-130. The chord series (Ex. 4a below) is interrupted by a figure, on trumpets and tympani, at measure 86 (Ex. 4b below):

Exx. 4a, 4b

Example 4b emphasizes the rhythmic pattern of Ex. 1. The chord series and rhythmic pattern (Exx. 4a and 4b) continue to alternate, but at measure 92 Ex. 4b assumes prime impor-

tance. The rhythmic figure continues unaccompanied, with the
addition of snare drum and bass drum, increases from a pianissimo to a fortissimo, and dies down again. Example 1
enters at measure 97, above the continuing rhythmic ostinato
of Ex. 4b.

The melodic line of Ex. 1 is introduced without its rhythmic
pattern, now assumed by the ostinato of Ex. 4b within its
texture. The passage builds to an agitated fortissimo, high-
lighted by the increasingly louder repetitions of Ex. 4b set
against orchestral figurations. The music suddenly halts at
measure 115, and Ex. 4b continues on alone, again building
from a pianissimo to a fortissimo. At measure 117 Exx. 4a
and 4b are superimposed contrapuntally and repeated in this
manner twice more, building to a triple forte at measure 124.
There is a gradual diminuendo, as Exx. 4a and 4b continue
quietly, subsiding to a few drum taps of Ex. 4b at measure
130.

CODA

Measures 130-142. At measure 130, Ex. 3 begins softly,
stated by solo English horn, and is joined by a quiet string
statement of Ex. 2 at measure 133. The English horn passage
quietly fades on a C-flat, under which Ex. 4b is softly heard
on tympani, bass drum and low pizzicato strings. The C-flat
leads without pause into the opening B-flat of the Scherzo,
so that these two movements are joined by the interval of
the semitone or minor second.

THIRD MOVEMENT

Form   Scherzo with repeated Trio
Section A   measures 1-109
Section B (Trio)   measures 110-239
Section A′   measures 240-306
Section B′ (Trio)   measures 307-371

SECTION A

Measures 1-109. The Scherzo begins with the motive of the augmented fourth, treated in canonic imitation. Each of the entrances appears at the fifth, in increasing rhythmic diminution, so that the main melodic line sounds as a series of augmented fourths separated by semitones:

Ex. 1

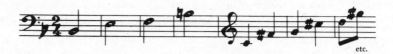

The cycle of augmented fourths reaches E by measure 8, and a new thematic figure appears in unison woodwinds. It, too, outlines an augmented fourth (bracketed below), alternating between the notes E and B-flat.

Ex. 2

Example 2 builds to a crescendo at measure 20, in which Exxs. 1 and 2 are combined contrapuntally, to be interrupted by another statement of Ex. 2 at measure 26. The expansion of Ex. 2, now veering between the notes E-flat and A, leads to a fortissimo restatement of Ex. 1 in rhythmically altered form. First appearing in the low brass, it is answered canonically throughout the orchestra and combined with fragments of Ex. 2, beginning at measure 35. The passage continues at a steady fortissimo level, and Ex. 2 begins to dominate the texture at measure 56, heard against a statement of Ex. 1 in augmentation at measure 64. Stated initially by trombones and tuba, this broad treatment of Ex. 1 is taken up by the horns at measure 74, against the steady figuration of Ex. 2. A descending stretto on Ex. 2 at measure 84 provides a background for the return of Ex. 1 in its original rhythmic form at measure 90, again imitated canonically. Example 2 is restated at measure 97, now veering between the notes C and F-sharp, as the music gradually subsides to a pianissimo.

SECTION B (TRIO)

Measures 110-170. Against a steady sixteenth-note ostinato and syncopated drum taps, the solo tenor saxophone introduces a new melody:

Ex. 3

etc.

The interval of the minor third alternates here with the semitone and the augmented fourth. After a broad statement of Ex. 3 by the solo saxophone, the theme is taken up by full orchestra at measure 126, fortissimo, and then diminishes in intensity. The saxophone takes up the theme at measure 145, and a sudden crescendo leads to another fortissimo statement of Ex. 3 by full orchestra, presented in high strings and winds over the continual sixteenth-note figuration in the lower registers, brass chords, cymbals and bass drum. The orchestral treatment, beginning at measure 155, gradually subsides in volume and is suddenly interrupted by a string tremolo at measure 170.

Measures 170-239. Solo bassoon quietly plays Ex. 1 in inversion, against the string tremolo, imitated by other winds against soft figurations and the string tremolo. Example 1 is added to this texture at measure 185, in its original ascending form but in rhythmic diminution. Example 1 proper appears at measure 193, in low brass, in counterpoint to its inversion, and leads to the inversion of Ex. 2 at measure 202, stated by strings against the inversion of Ex. 1 in augmentation. This passage is expanded sequentially and builds to a fortissimo at measure 224 which gradually subsides.

SECTION A'

Measures 240-306. At measure 240, the inversion of Ex. 1 appears softly in the lower registers, under an ostinato related to Ex. 2, and is answered canonically. A crescendo leads to a fortissimo statement of Ex. 2 at measure 248, no longer veering but ascending to a high A at measure 254. At this point Ex. 1 and its inversion, both in rhythmic augmentation, are contrapuntally set against a rushing sixteenth-note ostinato. At measure 284, Ex. 2 reappears in its original form, unison winds veering between the notes A-flat and D, and is expanded into a rushing sixteenth-note passage for strings and winds that suddenly reaches an abrupt pause at measure 306.

SECTION B' (TRIO)

Measures 307-371. Example 3 returns at measure 307, fortissimo, stated by full orchestra in rhythmic augmentation, and is immediately repeated, beginning at measure 331. The volume begins to subside at measure 347, and a rapid diminuendo leads to the quiet inversion of Ex. 1 stated by solo clarinets over tremolo strings at measure 352, punctuated by a fragment of Ex. 2 in inversion in low bassoons. The clarinet solo is taken up by bass clarinet, which dies away on a sustained low E leading directly into the final movement. As the Epilogue begins on the note F, these two movements are joined by a semitone.

FOURTH MOVEMENT (Epilogue)

Form	free "sectional" form
Section A	measures 1-38
Section B	measures 39-49
Section C	measures 49-73
Section D	measures 73-106

(summary of A, B, C)

This final movement is the true slow movement of the symphony and is unique in that the dynamic level remains pianissimo throughout its entirety, 106 measures in all. There is no definite formal or tonal scheme, and the tempo is uniform throughout. Thus the total effect of the movement is one of constant directionless flux. In Cooke's words, "the chief point about this movement is that *nothing happens*."[6]

The movement has been of special concern to those critics who have attempted an interpretation of the symphony. Dickinson feels that the Epilogue sets this symphony apart from all others and adds, "in determining to what the struggles of the previous three movements point, this epilogue may well symbolize a more penetrative reflection on our tragical discontents than an eloquent emotional intensity."[7] Scott Goddard comments, "the symphony closes without ending. All Vaughan Williams' symphonies end quietly, except the fourth . . . [but] this sixth differs from them all in that it ends on a question: Whither?"[8] And Howes offers an interpretation in support of his thesis that this is a "war" symphony, contending that the movement represents "aftermath . . . dead-sea fruit . . . the spiritual consequences of war."[9]

SECTION A

Measures 1-38. Muted violins present a lengthy theme, which contains within its contours many of the important features of the entire symphony.

Ex. 1

Note the consistent use of the minor third, semitone and augmented fourth, as well as the dot-dot-dash rhythm of the second movement. But, as a final irony, the combination of all these vital elements into one theme results in a melodic line utterly devoid of vitality.

The second violins enter above Ex. 1 with a variant of it at measure 4, followed by violas at measure 9 and 'celli at measure 13. The entrances are imitative and at intervals of semitones or augmented fourths from each other. At measure 22 the flutes enter with Ex. 1 in augmentation, while horns add a series of parallel chords to the texture. At measure 34, clarinets enter with Ex. 1 in augmentation but soon subside. The contrapuntal texture dies away to a brief silence at measure 39.

SECTION B

Measures 39-49. The silence is broken by a chord pattern, pianissimo in muted horns and low strings.

Ex. 2

Example 2 presents an F chord resolving to an E chord, and in this respect is related to the F-E clash of the opening movement (see measures 1-2, 188-192, first movement). Its statement here is answered by a rising figure in solo 'cello. Divided strings state Ex. 2 at measure 43, followed by an ascending pattern for clarinets and bass clarinet outlining a diminished chord (composed of two minor thirds, and outlining an augmented fourth). Ex. 2 is then stated once more by muted horns at measure 49.

SECTION C

Measures 49-73. At measure 49 the solo oboe begins a variant of Ex. 1 which involves much wider intervallic skips and rhythmic variety:

Ex. 3

In the context of the entire movement, this theme seems almost romantic; it is certainly less forbidding and inhuman than all that surrounds it. It is stated by oboe over a succession of parallel triads and then answered by clarinet and bass clarinet. Example 3 is expanded by unison strings, against woodwind and horn obbligato, and finally subsides in the low string registers.

SECTION D

Measures 73-106. Example 1 appears at measure 73, in high string tremolo, and is again answered imitatively by tremolo strings. An additional harp entrance in augmentation at measure 76 is followed by an entrance, in augmentation, of clarinet and bass clarinet at measure 80. The passage leads to a brief restatement of Ex. 2 in muted horns at measure 85, followed by the ascending diminished-chord pattern (heard previously at measure 45), expanded and treated imitatively throughout the string section. Example 3 appears on solo oboe, beginning at measure 94, and continues its descending triplet pattern until it fades on a low note E. Example 1 is once more stated at measure 99, in low pizzicato strings under alternately E-flat major and E minor chords. The E minor chord, in second inversion, is the last to be heard and is sustained until it dies away.

◆   ◆   ◆

Frank Howes discovered that Vaughan Williams, while working ' on this symphony, was simultaneously composing music for the film *Scott of the Antarctic,* which later developed into the *Sinfonia Antartica.* Believing that both the Sixth Symphony and the film score are concerned with "desolation," Howes raises the possibility that this similarity in mood may have resulted from an association of ideas when composition of the two works overlapped in 1947.

Ernest Irving, conductor of the film score and musical director of Ealing Film Studios, denied knowledge of any direct musical kinship between the two works, and the composer admitted no conscious awareness of any such relationship. Vaughan Williams did admit, however, that two of the symphony's themes — the opening themes of the second and fourth movements — had been derived from music for still another film, *The Flemish Farm.* However, the music for *The Flemish Farm* carried little connotation of either war or desolation. Perhaps one must conclude, then, that the symphony's extraordinary emotional impact lies not in the power of any particular themes, but in the context of the whole.[10]

Sinfonia Antartica, Number 7

IT WAS NOTED PREVIOUSLY that the *Sinfonia Antartica* had its origins in the incidental music for the film *Scott of the Antarctic*. Although the film music was written in 1947, the *Sinfonia* itself was not completed until 1952. It received its first performance early in 1953.

Howes reports that the original title of the work was *Sinfonia Antarctica*. The composer was subsequently informed that the two words were not linguistically compatible, one being a derivation from the Italian and the other from Greek. That is, the work might conceivably have been entitled *Sinfonia Antartica* or *Symphonia Antarctica,* but not a hybrid of the two. Vaughan Williams, admitting his linguistic lapse, chose the former of the two alternatives.[1]

A very large orchestra is called for, including piano, organ, a wordless female chorus, and such percussion as vibraphone, xylophone, glockenspiel, celesta and wind machine. There are five movements to the work, each of which is prefaced with a short literary quotation. Only the last of these quotations deals specifically with the Scott expedition to the Antarctic. the daring venture that proved unsuccessful.

FIRST MOVEMENT (Prelude)

Form	Sectional, in three parts
Section A	measures 1-56
Section B	measures 57-158
Section C	measures 159-203

To suffer woes which hope thinks infinite,
To forgive wrongs darker than death or night,

121

To defy power which seems omnipotent,
Neither to change, nor falter, nor repent:
This . . . is to be
Good, great, joyous, beautiful and free,
This is alone life, joy, empire and victory.

Shelley, *Prometheus Unbound*

SECTION A

Measures 1-56. The movement begins quietly with a statement of the main theme, which is to figure prominently in the last movement as well. The expansive melody is doubled throughout the orchestra and accompanied simply by major and minor triads in parallel motion:

Ex. 1

Example 1 is extended in a crescendo and then grows suddenly quiet at measure 15, building to another climax at measure 39. Again a sudden pianissimo statement of Ex. 1, now in two-voice stretto, is extended to a crescendo. A definite cadence, fortissimo, on the G major triad, is reached at measure 56.

SECTION B

Measures 57-93. There is an unexpected change in dynamics, to pianissimo, and a reduction in tempo. Soft tremolo and scale patterns on xylophone and piano produce an eerie ostinato, and a slow motive is stated over this ostinato at measure 59.

Ex. 2

Example 2, doubled in unison and octaves throughout the

orchestra, leads directly into another ostinato for brass and
ponticello tremolo strings at measure 68. A wordless soprano
solo and answering (wordless) female chorus enter immediately over this ostinato with a melodic variant of Ex. 2. As
the choral passage is expanded, the sounds of the wind machine
are heard, increasing in intensity and then fading away. At
measure 87 a fragment of Ex. 1 is briefly stated, pianissimo,
and then quickly subsides.

Measures 94-158. There is an increase in tempo, and
broken chords, arpeggios and scale figurations are quietly
stated by celesta, glockenspiel, vibraphone and piano, against
strings and woodwinds. This passage leads directly to an
agitated motive stated over a steady marching bass, beginning
at measure 105. This motive is similar in contour to Ex. 2.

With changed instrumentation, the motive is expanded over
an ostinato of percussion arpeggio and scale figurations. The
passage increases in intensity, reaching a fortissimo at measure
116, where a sharply rhythmic brass figure appears against
the ostinato of wind, percussion, string and harp figurations.
The music dies away and then increases again, building to
another fortissimo at measure 125. There is a sudden pianissimo at measure 126, and a rising melodic figure in the woodwinds leads to a new motive at measure 133, a series of two
chords with sharp rhythmic punctuations on the off-beats and
the added sonorities of deep bells:

Ex. 3

This pattern is repeated twice more, each time with increased volume, and the final fortissimo statement is interrupted by a return of the soprano solo passage at measure 141. The chorus and wind machine also reappear, increase in intensity, and then subside.

SECTION C

Measures 159-203. At measure 159, a trumpet fanfare appears. This may symbolize the first human element in the work, the appearance of man in the Antarctic desolation.

Ex. 4

· etc.

Example 4 is stated quietly by trumpets, as if from a distance, and is answered at measure 163 by a reference to Ex. 1, pianissimo, in low strings and winds. Example 4 is then repeated at measure 168 and grows in intensity, with increased instrumentation and contrapuntal texture. The gradual crescendo builds to a fortissimo statement of Ex. 1 at measure 184, again alternating with Ex. 4. Piano and harp glissandi are added to the orchestral texture. A final statement of Ex. 4, at measure 198, brings the music to a fortissimo on a held G major chord.

SECOND MOVEMENT (Scherzo)

Form   Scherzo and Trio
Section A   measures 1-80
Section B (Trio)   measures 81-137
Section A'   measures 137-152

There go the ships
and there is that Leviathan
whom thou hast made to take his pastime therein.
                                        Psalm 104

SECTION A

Measures 1-80. A quiet horn call and whole-tone scale flurries in low woodwinds and harp introduce the movement. A sudden crescendo leads to the restatement of the horn call at measure 9, now as a fanfare on full brass.

Ex. 1

A sudden cresendo and decrescendo lead to a melodic figure at measure 25.

Ex. 2

etc.

Both Ex. 1 and Ex. 2 are reminiscent of the Scherzo of the 1910 *Sea Symphony.*[2]

The rapid scale passages are now carried by strings, as Exx. 1 and 2 are extended by brass and wind. At measure 38, Ex. 2 is stated fully by strings against a solo horn obbligato and rapid wind figurations, but this passage is interrupted by a clarinet solo at measure 44, leading to an ostinato pattern of xylophone, celesta, piano and glockenspiel figurations, pizzicato and tremolo strings. An angular melodic figure in low woodwinds is set against this ostinato at measure 58, but its appearance is brief:

Ex. 3

The rushing ostinato figurations continue with ever greater force and reach a great climax at measure 74, at which point Exx. 1 and 2 are added to the texture, in fortissimo brass. The passage quickly subsides to a quiet string tremolo.

SECTION B (TRIO)

Measures 81-137. A new motive appears over the tremolo strings. This is an extended falling figure, covering more than two octaves. The emphasis is upon the augmented triad (compare with the use of the augmented fourth in Ex. 3 above):

Ex. 4

etc.

Howes remarks that both Exx. 3 and 4 appeared in the original film score; they represented, respectively, whales and penguins.[3]

Example 4 is accompanied by a repeated triplet figure and occasionally punctuated by bass drum and cymbal beats. The xylophone, beginning at measure 90, also aids in outlining the basic rhythmic pulse of the theme. Unexpectedly, beginning at measure 98, the triplet figures assume importance and are repeated with increasing intensity. This crescendo builds to a climax at measure 110, as Ex. 4 is presented fortissimo by low brass set against the incessant triplet figures which are now accentuated by cymbal crashes. The volume subsides gradually, and Ex. 4 is heard quietly at measure 122. The motive is finally stated, beginning at measure 133, by bassoons and tuba and fades into a fragment of Ex. 2 at measure 137, quietly presented by the violins.

SECTION A'

Measures 137-152. The restatement of Ex. 2 is set against a rushing scale passage in solo clarinet and gradually subsides to a held tone B-flat in high strings. Against this sustained tone, Ex. 1 is heard, pianissimo, in muted brass and celesta at measure 147, and softly dies away.

THIRD MOVEMENT (Landscape)

Form	Five-part Song
Section A	measures 1-55
Section B'	measures 56-90
Section C	measures 91-117
Section B'	measures 118-148
Section A'	measures 148-159

Ye ice falls! Ye that from the mountain's brow
Adown enormous ravines slopes amain —
Torrents, methinks, that once heard a mighty voice,
And stopped at once amid their maddest plunge!
Motionless torrents! Silent cataracts!

Coleridge, "Hymn before Sunrise,
in the Vale of Chamouni"

In this movement, the tendency towards sonorities for their own sake, used sporadically in earlier movements, becomes pronounced. Although thematic material is presented and extended through development or restatement, orchestral colors and sonorities *per se* command the greatest attention in the movement.

SECTION A

Measures 1-55. Against a background of quiet cymbal rolls, harp glissandi and high woodwind discords, a motive is presented by muted horns at measure 4:

Ex. 1

As Cooke has noted, in its emphasis on the rising and falling interval of the third, it resembles the main subject of the Epilogue of the Sixth Symphony.[4] The passage continues quietly, then subsides after a held tone.

At measure 22, a new ostinato pattern is established, consisting of rapid scale figurations in celesta, glockenspiel and
woodwinds against sustained chords and broken chords in
strings and piano. A brass motive, slowly descending and emphasizing the interval of the third, is set against this ostinato.
The dynamics are subdued throughout, creating a unity of
mood and texture, although the instrumentation of the ostinato is altered at measure 32 and the tempo quickens at
measure 44. Suddenly, at measure 50, a loud crash of the
gong brings the music to a sharp climax, as descending major
thirds are stated throughout the orchestra, culminating in a
fortissimo A-flat tone on all instruments. This is held, then
gradually diminishes.

SECTION B

Measures 56-90. A slow but steadily moving melodic line,
almost devoid of rhythmic activity, is presented at measure 56.
A stretto-like imitative voice is added after little more than
a measure, and the two voices proceed slowly and quietly.
Low tones on piano and organ pedal, and high flute and
piccolo, outline the outermost octaves.

Ex. 2

The melodic lines accentuate rising and falling augmented
fourths, and their combination in counterpoint results in strong
dissonances. As Cooke noted in a comparison of this passage
with the last two movements of the Sixth Symphony, tonality
is also weakened through the use of the augmented fourth.[5]
A soft stroke of the gong introduces a new motive at

V-288

Bridge Street, summer at VAIL, COLORADO.

Photographed and Published by R.C. Bishop, P.O. 1177, Grand Junction, Colo. 81501

Printed in Spain

measure 65, a short melodic figure harmonized in parallel major triads:

Ex. 3

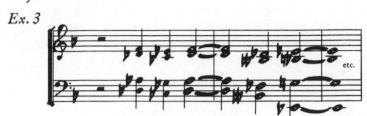

Example 3 is first heard in horns and low winds, and then expanded with the addition of the full wind choir. At measure 76, Ex. 2 reappears, again in two-voice stretto, and quietly leads to a fragment of Ex. 3 on muted brass, beginning at measure 83. Example 1 is heard softly above it on solo flute, at measure 85, and the flute passage continues against the repeated fragment of Ex. 3.

SECTION C

Measures 91-117. A slight alteration of contour at the conclusion of the flute statement, beginning at measure 89, is now expanded into an elaborate melodic line:

Ex. 4

Heard first in low strings against a delicate accompaniment of woodwinds and harp, Ex. 4 is repeated at measure 103 with added doubling of violins, oboe, English horn and bassoon, and then begins to subside at measure 115.

SECTION B'

Measures 118-148. There is a sudden crescendo leading to

a fortissimo restatement of Ex. 2 at measure 118. This passage builds rapidly in intensity and is climaxed by the appearance of Ex. 3 as an organ solo at measure 127. The fortissimo solo is set against great sweeps of the harp, piano and strings, and does not diminish in volume until measure 141. Example 3 is then softly restated by brasses and harp, against a fragment of Ex. 4 in high strings and winds.

SECTION A'

Measures 148-159. At measure 148, Ex. 1 is heard on muted trumpets against its original background of cymbals, harp glissandi and high woodwinds. Example 4 has now been incorporated into the melodic line. The trumpet passage diminishes and subsides on a sustained note F, which leads directly into the next movement.

FOURTH MOVEMENT (Intermezzo)

Form	Three-part Song
Section A	measures 1-81
Section B	measures 82-111
Section A'	measures 112-131

Love, all alike, no season knows, nor clime,
Nor hours, days, months, which are the rags of time.
Donne, "The Sun Rising"

SECTION A

Measures 1-36. Against a quiet accompaniment of harp chords, the solo oboe presents a broad theme at measure 5, stressing the alternately major and minor inflection of the third scale degree:

Ex. 1

Ex. 1, which is immediately taken up by other winds and strings at measure 13, acquires great intensity through contrapuntal imitation and abrupt changes in dynamics. The melody is again stated quietly by the solo oboe at measure 22 but is once more expanded to a full tutti. This passage gradually subsides to a brief English horn solo at measure 34.

Measures 37-81. An increase in tempo occurs at measure 37, and a new theme is introduced.

Ex. 2

Although Ex. 2 is in 4/4 meter, it is similar in contour and mood to Ex. 1. Solo violin is added to the texture at measure 42, and solo 'cello at measure 52, while solo flute and oboe also appear at measure 50. As the melodic lines become highly florid, these voices are heard in combination and separately in imitation. The passage subsides on a descending figure, and Ex. 2 is stated simply and quietly by horns at measure 66, then by strings at measure 71. As winds and brasses are added to the texture, the music builds to a gradual climax at measure 80, followed by a sudden diminuendo.

SECTION B

Measures 82-111. At measure 82, there is an unexpected reappearance of Ex. 3 of the opening movement, complete with deep bells and off-beat rhythmic punctuation. The motive does not increase in volume with repetition, however, but remains pianissimo throughout. It is interrupted, at measure 89, by a succession of repeated chords on divided strings, and by a woodwind figure at measure 94:

Ex. 3

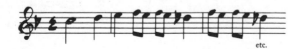

Example 3 is a variant of Ex. 1 of the opening movement. The repeated chords appear again at measure 96 and are answered by Ex. 3, which is extended through contrapuntal imitation. The passage subsides to a quiet restatement of the "bell" motive[6] at measure 108.

SECTION A'

Measures 112-131. After a brief silence, Ex. 1 is stated by solo oboe and then combined in canon with other solo woodwinds against the chords of the harp. The melody is taken up by the strings at measure 118 and subsides on a sustained F-sharp on 'celli and quiet pizzicati chords of B (minus the third).

FIFTH MOVEMENT (Epilogue)

Form	March with Trio
Section A	measures 1-51
Section B (Trio)	measures 52-87
Section A'	measures 88-129
Coda	measures 130-190

> I do not regret this journey; we took risks, we knew we took them, things have come out against us, therefore we have no cause for complaint.
>
> Captain Scott's last journal

SECTION A

Measures 1-51. Against a fortissimo tremolo in strings and winds, the trumpets state the opening theme of the movement, similar in contour and rhythm to Ex. 5 of the opening movement:

Ex. 1

etc.

Still against the tremolo, Ex. 1 is transferred to horns at
measure 7 and then treated in stretto by full brass, beginning
at measure 11. The tremolo diminishes, leading to a tutti statement, at measure 19, of Ex. 3 of the Intermezzo, doubled in
unison and octave against marching brass chords. This theme,
as previously noted, is a variant of Ex. 1 of the Prelude.
Although no example is given here, the theme will be referred
to in this movement as Ex. 2.

At measure 24, Ex. 1 is again treated in stretto in horns and
trumpets against string and wind tremolo, followed immediately by a fragment of Ex. 2 set against a syncopated marching bass. At measures 33 and 40, Ex. 1 is briefly set against
this steady march, in each instance as the climax of a sudden
crescendo.

A new motive appears at measure 43, still against the
marching bass line:

Ex. 3

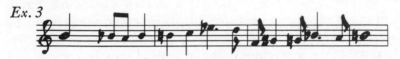

It appears at a fortissimo and then gradually diminishes in
intensity. The march-like accompaniment figure also subsides,
ending at measure 50, replaced by a descending scale passage,
pianissimo.

SECTION B (Trio)

Measures 52-87. An ostinato pattern is introduced at
measure 52, consisting of open fifths on piano and harp and
a variant of Ex. 2 in low clarinet and bass clarinet. Triplets,
two to a bar of 4/4, are added to the ostinato pattern and
become increasingly important as the passage continues:

Against the ostinato, a melodic figure is stated by solo bassoon at measure 67, and is then taken up by strings and winds at measure 76. A gradual crescendo is climaxed by a fortissimo reiteration of the triplet pattern,[7] beginning at measure 84, and quickly subsiding.

SECTION A'

Measures 88-129. Example 3 quietly reappears, once more set against a marching bass. At a sudden fortissimo, Ex. 2 is heard in stretto at measure 96; it grows in intensity, to be interrupted by the "bell" motive, pianissimo, at measure 105. Against a string tremolo, the wordless female chorus and wind machine of the Prelude enter at measure 111. A sudden crescendo leads to the restatement of Ex. 1 against the string tremolo and wind machine at measure 114, and the chorus again enters, after an equally abrupt diminuendo, at measure 119. Example 1, the chorus and wind machine alternate briefly as the passage continues to diminish in volume. Example 1 is finally stated, pianissimo, over tympani and cymbal rolls, gradually dying away.

CODA

Measures 130-190. The tempo and meter revert to that of the Prelude, and Ex. 1 of the Prelude, in its original form, appears at measure 130. The motive is expanded and extended as in the opening movement, building to a fortissimo at measure 162. A gradual diminuendo leads to a restatement·

of the quiet soprano solo of the Prelude above a pedal G in low strings, beginning at measure 173. Over this continuing pedal, the soprano, female chorus and wind machine are heard briefly and then subside into silence.

❖   ❖   ❖

It is debatable whether or not this work falls into the category of symphony. Howes suggests that it was entitled *Sinfonia* to indicate that, in programmatic implications, it stands somewhere between a symphony and a symphonic poem.[8] The work's most positive features, i.e. textures and sonorities of individual passages, are not strictly symphonic attributes. On the other hand, Colin Mason, who regards the two outer movements as the most symphonic, states that "the composer has made a work which stands firmly on its own formal and musical merits, as real a symphony as Beethoven's 'Pastoral.' "[9]

The literary quotations at the head of each movement are certainly indicative of a program more explicit than the usual symphonic scheme. But even if these prefaces had been deleted from the final score, as was the quotation from Bunyan in the Fifth Symphony, much of the music *per se* would reveal its symbolic, representational nature. The reliance upon texture, sonority and tone-painting, and the formal divisions into many brief sections, as well as the recurrence of entire passages throughout the work, strongly suggest the presence of a narrative which does not have its basis in musical logic alone.

These factors should not be considered detrimental to the work. They were fully acknowledged, or at least indicated, by the composer, and are thus in no way accidental. Moreover, they represent the natural outcome of an extended work which had its beginnings in purely descriptive music, but which transcends these beginnings. As Michael Kennedy remarks, speaking of Vaughan Williams in 1957, "of the unchecked activity of his eighties, 'Sinfonia Antartica' is the most original and powerful product."[10]

Symphony in D Minor, Number 8

THE SYMPHONY IN D MINOR OF 1956 is noticeably different from its predecessors in its diminutive scale and comparatively short length. Dickinson speaks of its "symphonically lighter touch,"[1] and Ottaway notes that it does not have "the visionary concentration, the total absorption in a particular facet of experience, which characterizes each of Vaughan Williams' symphonies since the 'Pastoral' . . . accordingly, it is not susceptible to literary description in quasi-mystical terms!"[2]

Like the *Sinfonia Antartica,* the Symphony in D minor is scored for an unusually large percussion ensemble, including vibraphone, xylophone, glockenspiel, tubular bells, tuned gongs and celesta. The remaining orchestration, however, is comparatively slight: horns, trumpets and woodwinds in twos, three trombones which are silent for much of the symphony, strings and tympani.

FIRST MOVEMENT (Variazioni senza Tema)

Form	Variations (Sonata-Allegro)
Variations 1-3 (Exposition)	measures 1-139
Variations 4, 5 (Development)	measures 140-212
Variations 6, 7 (Recapitulation)	measures 213-284

This movement actually bears the title "Fantasia," plus the added comment, "Variazioni senza Tema." The composer in his own program notes speaks of the movement as "seven variations in search of a theme," but admits the possibility of interpreting the scheme in terms of the traditional Sonata-Allegro form. Day also states that the movement can "by dint of a little loose definition of terms . . . be analysed in

terms of a sonata movement."[3] The present analysis, however, will deal with the movement as a series of variations.

VARIATION 1

Measures 1-44. The main subject of the opening movement
is a four note figure, a pair of rising fourths.

Ex. 1

Example 1 is immediately stated by solo trumpet and horn
against a quiet accompaniment of vibraphone, celesta and
pizzicato strings. An answering figure, which again stresses
fourths, appears on solo flute at measure 9 and is then taken
up by clarinets and bassoon at measure 16:

Ex. 2

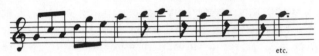

A new motive appears, fortissimo in strings, at measure 22.
A hemiola rhythmic relationship between the melody and bass
line adds to the intensity of the passage.

Ex. 3

Example 3 is extended in a crescendo, which leads to a restatement of Ex. 1 at measure 34. Example 2 follows immediately, suddenly quiet, at measure 35, stated by solo flute

against vibraphone and celesta and then answered by solo
bassoon. The quiet passage subsides on brief statements
of Ex. 1 by solo trumpet and horn, beginning at measure 42.

VARIATION 2

Measures 45-107. The tempo changes to Presto, and a
rapidly ascending figure begins in the strings at measure 45,
answered by sharp accents in woodwinds and triangle. Example 4 is based upon Ex. 1, although one of the fourths has
become augmented:

Ex. 4

At measure 50, reference to Ex. 2 appears over this pattern
in oboe and horn, followed by an expansion of Ex. 4 treated
imitatively between strings and winds and building to a climax
at measure 62. After a sudden diminuendo and another crescendo, a variant of Ex. 3 appears at measure 73, again
stressing rhythmic hemiola. Example 1, in glockenspiel, high
winds and pizzicato strings, appears briefly at measure 79
and is immediately answered by another variant of Ex. 3 at
measure 83. Examples 1 and 3 again alternate, leading to
a rushing passage reminiscent of Ex. 4. The passage grows
in intensity, reaching a climax at measure 107 and then coming
to an abrupt stop.

VARIATION 3

Measures 108-139. After a moment of silence, the music
resumes at a much slower tempo, in 4/4 meter. One of its
fourths now a perfect fifth, Ex. 1 is heard in the low strings,
set against a countersubject in a higher register:

Ex. 5

Although the C major triad is prominently featured, the tonality seems to be A-Aeolian. At measure 114 another variant of Ex. 1 appears in solo flute, oboe and 'cello, which definitely establishes A-Aeolian.

Ex. 6

Example 6 is developed contrapuntally by strings and winds and then subsides to another statement of Ex. 5 at measure 128 for strings, set against a fragment of Ex. 6 for solo clarinet. The quiet passage is interrupted by a vigorous restatement of Ex. 3, which quickly fades into silence.

VARIATION 4

Measures 140-182. In 6/8 meter, solo oboe presents an extended melody, reminiscent of both Exx. 1 and 2 and at a slightly faster tempo.

Ex. 7

After three measures, the melody is imitated contrapuntally by solo clarinet and then taken up by bassoons and brasses

(minus trombones, which have not yet appeared in the movement). The brass version of Ex. 7, beginning at measure 151,
is set in 2/4 meter, establishing a hemiola against the prevailing 6/8, and leads to the entrance of Ex. 3 at measure 158,
its 6/8 set against Ex. 7 in 2/4. A short crescendo builds to
a climax at measure 167 and then gradually subsides to a
quiet restatement of the movement's opening celesta and vibraphone figure, now scored for winds and harp, at measure
181.

VARIATION 5

Measures 183-212. Another variant of Ex. 1 appears,
after a brief silence, at measure 183. In 4/4 meter, the series
of fourths is extended and rises from the low string register to
high brasses and winds:

Ex. 8

A variant of Ex. 2 soon follows, at measure 192, stated first
by solo oboe and then imitated by other winds, finally taken
up by strings at measure 198 against a variant of Ex. 3. As
Ex. 1 in horns and trumpets is added to the texture, the passage gradually increases in intensity, and the crescendo reaches
a fortissimo at measure 210.

VARIATION 6

Measures 213-236. The crescendo leads directly to a rapid
restatement of Ex. 1 in 6/8 meter, similar in tempo, orches-

tration and mood to Ex. 4. Against scale figurations in high winds and the rapid version of Ex. 1, horns and trumpets state a martial motive emphasizing augmented fourths and fifths. The side drum and triangle add rhythmic emphasis, as the passage remains at a forte dynamic level. A variant of Ex. 2 appears in strings and winds at measure 225, again stressing augmented fourths, and a short crescendo begins.

VARIATION 7

Measures 237-284. At the height of the crescendo there is a sudden silence and then a return to the slower tempo and 4/4 meter of Variation 3. Example 5 is stated softly by winds and brasses against a fragment of Ex. 8 in strings. Example 8 persists as an ostinato, as Ex. 6 is stated by high winds and brasses at measure 242, developed contrapuntally in an extended crescendo. The passage is climaxed by the restatement of Ex. 5, fortissimo in D major, at measure 252. At this point the trombones make their first entrance in the movement. After a second fortissimo statement of Ex. 5 at measure 256, the passage gradually subsides to a pianissimo. In 6/8 meter, Ex. 2 is heard softly on solo woodwinds at measure 268, answered by Ex. 1 on muted solo brass and the opening accompaniment figure of vibraphone and celesta. The movement quietly fades on a held D minor triad in strings.

SECOND MOVEMENT (Scherzo Alla Marcia)
(per stromenti a fiato)

Form	Scherzo (March) and Trio
Section A	measures 1-126
Section B (Trio)	measures 127-153
Section A'	measures 154-181

As its title indicates, this movement is scored only for woodwind and brass instruments.

SECTION A

Measures 1-81. A march-like rhythmic ostinato is established by oboes, clarinets and muted high brasses. Against this ostinato pattern a melody appears in the bassoons at measure 5. In C minor, its lowered second degree lends it a Phrygian character:

Ex. 1

The melody is taken up by flute and piccolo at measure 22, leading to another march-like accompaniment figure in low brass and a trumpet solo at measure 36.

Ex. 2

Example 2 is immediately repeated, beginning at measure 46, and leads to still another theme, a melody for flute and piccolo at measure 54 set against more syncopated accompaniment in low winds and horns.

Ex. 3

Example 3 is answered by a rhythmic clarinet figure,

Ex. 4

and Exx. 3 and 4 alternate in an increasing crescendo. The passage builds to a fortissimo climax at measure 74, in which

Ex. 3 is stated in stretto imitation between trombones and horns against a running sixteenth-note pattern reminiscent of Ex. 1, in woodwinds. This passage rapidly subsides, reaching a pianissimo at measure 81.

Measures 82-126. A quiet bassoon statement of Ex. 4, beginning at measure 82, is treated as a fugue subject, answered by clarinets at measure 87 and high winds at measure 94. Trumpets enter at measure 100 and horns at measure 105, and a crescendo leads to a fortissimo statement of the subject in rhythmic augmentation at measure 109, repeated at measure 117 against the subject in its original rhythmic form. There is a rapid diminuendo, leading to a pianissimo at measure 126.

SECTION B (TRIO)

Measures 127-153. A new melody is introduced by low woodwinds, in 6/8 meter and at a slower tempo:

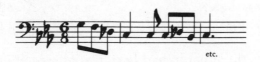

After its initial statement in the low registers of clarinet and bassoon, the theme is answered by solo flute against a quiet harmonic accompaniment at measure 136 and is finally taken up by solo oboe at measure 146 against a counterpoint of flute and clarinet. The oboe solo quietly subsides on a sustained low C.

SECTION A'

Measures 154-181. Against the held oboe tone, the opening march-like ostinato begins in high winds, answered by horns and trumpets, and once more in 2/4 meter. The rhythmic pattern suddenly increases in volume, with added instrumentation, and leads to a fortissimo stretto imitation, including rhythmic augmentation, of the fugal subject built on Ex. 4:

The passage rapidly grows quiet, and the movement ends un-expectedly, after a brief silence, on a pianissimo woodwind figure.

THIRD MOVEMENT (Cavatina)
(per stromenti ad arco)

Form	Sonatine
Exposition	measures 1-55
Interlude	measures 56-82
Recapitulation	measures 83-111

Note that the Scherzo had been placed second in the order of the four movements of the symphony and that this third movement is the "slow" movement. It is scored only for strings.

EXPOSITION

Measures 1-55. The movement begins with a lyric melody for 'celli, accompanied by occasional pianissimo chords and pizzicato bass:

Ex. 1

Note the extensive range of the melodic line and the use of duple and triple rhythms.

The high strings take up the melody at measure 13 but do not state it fully until measure 19, where it is set against a moving pizzicato scale-wise bass figure. A slight crescendo reaches a climax at measure 29 and then subsides to silence.

A second theme is introduced at measure 32, now in 3/4 meter.

Ex. 2

etc.

In contrast to the earlier contrapuntal texture of the movement, this melody is set simply in block chords, with the prominent G of the melody harmonized alternately with E-flat major or E minor triads. Violas and 'celli are doubled, increasing the harmonic texture to seven parts. The passage is pianissimo throughout.

INTERLUDE

Measures 56-82. The meter reverts to 4/4, and a variant of Ex. 1 is stated by violins against 'cello and divided violas, leading to an extended passage for solo violin at measure 63. The solo is heard against a viola tremolo background and punctuated by quiet pizzicati. A gradual crescendo is climaxed by a fortissimo passage in two-part counterpoint for the entire string section, at measure 72, which subsides to another florid violin solo, now unaccompanied.

RECAPITULATION

Measures 83-111. The conclusion of the violin solo leads directly to the restatement of Ex. 1 at measure 83, quietly presented by low strings and answered by a pianissimo figure in a higher register. The motive is developed contrapuntally, rhythmic duplets against triplets, and builds to a fortissimo at measure 94, followed by a gradual diminuendo.

After a brief pause, Ex. 2 is quietly stated by divided strings
at measure 97, subsiding to a sustained C-sharp minor chord
against which solo 'cello elaborates upon a florid variant of
Ex. 1. At the conclusion of the solo, the movement ends
quietly on a sustained chord of E major.

FOURTH MOVEMENT (Toccata)

Form	Rondo (Third Rondo)
Section A	measures 1-59
Section B	measures 59-95
Section A'	measures 95-104
Section C	measures 105-132
Section A''	measures 133-144
Section D	measures 145-175
Section A'''	measures 176-222

In this final movement the enlarged percussion forces of
the orchestra are used more extensively. Among the instruments employed are vibraphone, xylophone, celesta, glockenspiel, bells and gongs, as well as the more standard drums,
cymbals and tympani.

SECTION A

Measures 1-59. After a loud stroke of the gong and bell,
the first motive of the movement is stated by full orchestra,
alternating with a similar statement on all tuned percussion.

Ex. 1

A second motive, an extended variant of the first, appears

at measure 19 and is also passed between tuned percussion and full orchestra.

Ex. 2

A more lyric, extended variation of the same basic motive is presented by strings and winds at measure 29, against a running sixteenth-note figuration:

Ex. 3

A gradual crescendo, built upon Ex. 3 and its increasingly prominent rapid accompaniment, leads to a fortissimo tutti statement of Ex. 1 at measure 42, followed by Ex. 2 on glockenspiel, bells and gongs at measure 48 and then by a fortissimo cadence in D major which quickly subsides.

SECTION B

Measures 59-95. At measure 59, a lyric figure is quietly stated by violins against a repeated woodwind figure.

Ex. 4

The figure is then taken up by flute at measure 69 and, after a short crescendo and diminuendo, by harp and solo clarinet against vibraphone chords at measure 81. Celesta is added to the orchestral texture at measure 87, and a fragment of Ex. 4 is developed to a fortissimo at measure 92.

SECTION A'

Measures 95-104. The crescendo is climaxed by the return of Exx. 1 and 2 at measure 95, featuring brass, low winds and tuned percussion against string tremolo.

SECTION C

Measures 105-132. The brief restatement of Exx. 1 and 2 leads directly to a passage of rapid figurations, beginning at measure 105, alternating between woodwinds and pizzicato strings. A slower brass motive is set against this pattern and develops into an extended melodic line for full orchestra at measure 120, building to a climax at measure 128. Xylophone, cymbals and gongs are added to the texture.

SECTION A''

Measures 133-144. The passage suddenly diminishes in volume, and at measure 133 Ex. 1 is heard, in rhythmic augmentation, on glockenspiel, bells and gongs, followed immediately by a fragment of Ex. 2 in an increasing crescendo. A fortissimo at measure 141 involves rapid eighth-note figurations alternated antiphonally between high and low registers and employs all the percussion instruments.

SECTION D

Measures 145-175. The music suddenly becomes quiet, and a rising figure in low strings and harp, emphasizing the interval of the perfect fourth, is set against rapid woodwind figurations. The rising figure is passed to vibraphone at measure 155 and then to celesta and harp at measure 159, treated as an ascending series of parallel major triads against the rapid ostinato. High winds and trumpets present a variant of this motive, still emphasizing fourths, at measure 163, as the volume gradually increases and the rapid ostinato grows in prominence.

SECTION A'''

Measures 176-222. At measure 176, the glockenspiel, bells, harp and celesta sustain an ostinato of fortissimo glissandi, against which Ex. 3 is heard in low strings and brass, punctuated by fortissimo strokes of gong and cymbals. At measure 183 a sixteenth-note figuration in winds and strings is added to this texture, and Ex. 3 appears in the high registers, building to a great climax at measure 192 in which Exx. 1 and 2 are heard in glockenspiel, bells and gongs against a brass countersubject.

The fortissimo passage stops unexpectedly and then continues at measure 207, in a rapid passage involving stretto imitation of a variant of Exx. 1 and 2. This, too, comes to an abrupt halt.

At measure 216, Ex. 1 is stated for the final time by full orchestra, fortissimo and at a much slower tempo, reaching a definite cadence on a D major chord.

❖   ❖   ❖

The smaller scale of this work does not necessarily indicate that the symphony is inferior to its predecessors or that it represents any less creative vigor on the composer's part. Although the symphony does not present a single, concentrated mood or point of view throughout, its more heterogeneous qualities and effective contrasts are reminiscent of the earlier *A London Symphony*. The innovations in orchestration are obvious in this work, and it is always unusual to witness a composer experimenting with forms new to him at such an advanced stage in his career. The Eighth Symphony is, therefore, a highly imaginative work — perhaps even an experimental one — if not one of major proportions.

It should be noted, however, that this symphony is retrospective as well as experimental. It presents, in its many contrasting sections, varied stylistic features of the composer's earlier works in concise juxtaposition. Kennedy, in speaking of this symphony as a synthesis of many earlier phases, states that Vaughan Williams "has fused the varied features of his music into what amounts to a new style, no less fresh and direct than his youthful manner."[4]

The listener will find ample references to and reminders of the street cries of *A London Symphony,* the biting fourths of the Fourth Symphony, the simple, modal style of the Fifth Symphony, the alternating major-minor tensions of the Sixth Symphony, the preoccupation with orchestral color and sonority of the *Sinfonia Antartica.*

Since its first performance, the Eighth Symphony has become one of Vaughan Williams' most frequently programmed works, especially in the United States. It seems very likely, at this writing, that this symphony, like the *Fantasia on a Theme of Thomas Tallis,* will serve to keep its composer's name in the popular repertory and thus perhaps stimulate further interest in his major works.

Symphony in E Minor, Number 9

THE COMPOSER'S LAST SYMPHONY was completed late in 1957 and first performed in April, 1958. Vaughan Williams' death, in August, 1958, occurred on the eve of the recording of this work by the London Philharmonic Orchestra. He had planned to attend the recording session the following morning.

The scoring of the Symphony in E Minor, Number 9, is unusual, calling for a large orchestra that includes three saxophones and a flugelhorn as well as the augmented percussion section employed in the *Sinfonia Antartica* and the Eighth Symphony.

FIRST MOVEMENT

Form	Sonata-Allegro
Exposition	measures 1-102
Development	measures 102-133
Recapitulation	measures 134-181

EXPOSITION

Measures 1-39. After a held unison E, a slow theme is stated by low brasses and winds, set against the sustained E. While E is stressed as the keynote, the actual scale outlined is closer to that of F major-minor.

Ex. 1

The theme is imitated contrapuntally at the fifth, by higher winds and brasses at measure 7, and the passage subsides to a sustained E minor chord in divided strings, against which a chordal figure is stated by the saxophone choir:

Ex. 2

etc.

The F major-E minor relationship of this figure, termed a "Neapolitan" motive by the composer in his own program notes, heightens the F-E semitonal relationship implied in Ex. 1. This saxophone passage leads directly to a restatement of Ex. 1 at measure 16, set against triplet figurations (2 to a bar of 4/4). Example 1 is answered imitatively at the fifth at measure 20 and then imitated again by high strings and winds at measure 22. A gradual crescendo, emphasizing the triplet pattern, reaches a fortissimo at measure 28 and then rapidly diminishes in volume.

The solo clarinet states a new theme at measure 32, which again stresses the interval of the semitone, now in the context of an alternately major-minor third scale degree. The melody is accompanied simply with harp chords.

Ex. 3

A second solo clarinet enters imitatively at measure 34, followed by bass clarinet at measure 36. The florid three-voice counterpoint is still set against simple harp chords.

Measures 40-102. High strings and winds present a lyric melodic line at measure 40, imitated canonically a measure later.

Ex. 4

Example 4 is stated with more intensity at measure 45, and a rapid crescendo reaches a fortissimo climax at measure 52, as Ex. 1 is set in low brasses against an expanded treatment of Ex. 4. The passage is brought to an abrupt silence, followed by a richly scored statement of Ex. 3 at measure 57, which is extended through sequential treatment of its descending triplet figure. Against a sustained high B in strings and a triplet figuration for woodwinds at measure 73, appears a quiet statement of Ex. 2, in modified form, by brasses. A rapid crescendo leads to a third statement of Ex. 3, fortissimo and treated in modified stretto, at measure 81. Example 3 is again expanded through rising sequences, built upon its descending semitone figure, and an increasingly contrapuntal texture. The passage gradually increases in intensity, climaxed by rapid sixteenth-note figurations for all strings and winds.

DEVELOPMENT

Measures 102-133. The crescendo builds to a fortissimo at measure 102 and a tutti passage involving rapid triplet figurations and stressing semitones. This triplet pattern rapidly subsides to a quiet ostinato, against which Ex. 1 appears in the low register at measure 108, imitated at the fifth at measure 109. Example 2 is added to the texture at measure 112, first stated by horns and then by saxophones. A sudden crescendo builds to an intense statement of the triplet figures, in still increasing crescendo. The passage is abruptly halted at measure 124, and, after a brief silence, Ex. 4 is stated, fortissimo, harmonized by triads in parallel motion for full orchestra. The passage builds to another fortissimo at measure 129, in two-voice stretto, and then rapidly diminishes to silence.

RECAPITULATION

Measures 134-181. At measure 134, Ex. 3 is played quietly by solo violin against a chordal accompaniment of harp and pizzicato strings and then is stated by unison strings against a pianissimo flugelhorn countersubject and the harp chords. There is a brief silence at measure 157, followed by a sustained E for strings and a restatement of Ex. 1 by solo English horn, imitated at the fifth by solo horn as the strings revert to a modified Ex. 3 in unison and octave doublings. At measure 170, Ex. 1 is stated by flute and strings, now modified to an ascending Phrygian scale and resolving upon a sustained E minor triad. Against this triad, the saxophones restate Ex. 2 at measure 174. As Ex. 2 subsides, the movement closes quietly on the held E minor triad for divided strings.

SECOND MOVEMENT

Form	Song with repeated Trio
Section A	measures 1-54
Section B	measures 54-106
Section A'	measures 106-135
Section B'	measures 136-162

SECTION A

Measures 1-54. A lengthy flugelhorn solo opens the movement,

Ex. 1

followed immediately by a more rapid, march-like figure at measure 8, sharply accented and harmonized in parallel minor triads:

Ex. 2

The two motives alternate in increasing crescendo, leading to a fortissimo statement of Ex. 2 at measure 17, which subsides to a quiet presentation of Ex. 1 for low winds and flugelhorn at measure 23. Example 2 is then expanded, beginning at measure 27, with the addition of a rhythmic countersubject in strings and the punctuation of triangle and tenor drum. A gradual increase in intensity, followed by a rapid diminuendo, lead to a restatement of Ex. 1 at measure 48, scored for flugelhorn and low clarinets against a sustained B-flat minor triad for pianissimo divided strings.

SECTION B

Measures 54-106. At measure 54, a new melody is heard, stated at first by divided strings and then continued by solo oboe at measure 61:

Ex. 3

etc.

Example 3 is expanded and builds to an intense statement at measure 90, in which the third scale degree is alternately inflected major and minor. The crescendo continues to grow, with the addition of low brasses and harp to the texture, climaxed by a fortissimo at measure 103 which rapidly diminishes.

SECTION A'

Measures 106-135. A quiet stroke of the gong and deep bell introduce Ex. 1, stated softly by trombones and flugelhorn against a fragment of Ex. 3 in tremolo strings. A sudden crescendo leads to a fortissimo stroke of the gong and bell at measure 117 and the reappearance of Ex. 2, complete with its vigorous countersubject. Rhythm is now emphasized by cymbals and bass drum. The intensity gradually diminishes to a pianissimo at measure 130, as Ex. 2 is quietly stated by horns and then unison trombones, subsiding to silence.

SECTION B'

Measures 136-162. After a pianissimo stroke of the bell and gong, Ex. 3 is quietly stated by solo 'cello and muted strings, with the addition of woodwinds and harp at measure 146. The passage quietly subsides to a restatement of Ex. 1 on flugelhorn, set against pianissimo divided string chords which are alternately B-flat major and minor. Unexpectedly, however, the movement closes on a sustained chord of C major.

THIRD MOVEMENT (Scherzo)

Form	Scherzo and Trio
Section A	measures 1-199
Section B (Trio)	measures 200-267
Section A'	measures 268-308

SECTION A

Measures 1-79. After an opening fortissimo brass discord, accompanied by a rhythmic pattern on the side drum, the saxophones state the main theme of the movement, beginning at measure 6:

Ex. 1

The semitone is used as an alternating major-minor third scale degree, a device that recurs through all movements of this work.

The motive is taken up by the xylophone at measure 18, against a woodwind triplet figuration, and the passage leads to a new motive, stated at measure 25 by full orchestra.

Ex. 2

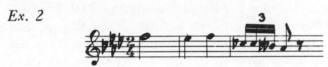

The triplet figure of Ex. 2 is expanded to a fortissimo, with the addition of side drum and tympani, and then rapidly subsides in volume. Still another motive is introduced at measure 42, stated by high winds over a rhythmic, march-like bass:

Ex. 3

Here the augmented fourth and perfect fourth alternate. Example 3 is expanded by full orchestra, including xylophone and glockenspiel, with added emphases on triangle and tympani and occasional saxophone obbligato. The passage leads to a fortissimo at measure 60, in which duple rhythms in winds and pizzicati strings are set against triple rhythms in brass, building to another statement of Ex. 3 in unison strings against saxophone figurations. Example 3 is taken up by the high woodwinds at measure 68, and the conflict of duple and triple rhythms resumes, now growing in intensity.

Measures 80-143. In 2/4 meter, a new motive is introduced, fortissimo, by strings, low winds and brass.

Ex. 4

References to Ex. 1, in 6/8, alternate with Ex. 4, continuing
the hemiola pattern, as duplet figures in ascending perfect
fourths are juxtaposed against triplet repeated-note patterns.
A rapid crescendo builds to a vigorous statement of Exx. 1
and 4 in counterpoint, beginning at measure 101. Example 4
is presented in canonic imitation as well. This three-voice
counterpoint builds to a fortissimo at measure 116, in which
triplet patterns in 6/8 are set against descending perfect
fourths in 2/4. The passage gradually subsides to a restatement of Ex. 1 at measure 126, now a fugato for the three
saxophones. Each entrance is punctuated by taps of the side
drum, and pizzicati strings are added to the texture at measure 138.

Measures 144-199. Example 3, stated at measure 144, is
set against a fragment of Ex. 1 at measure 147 and leads to
a restatement of Ex. 2 at measure 159, in high woodwinds
and unison strings. The passage builds to a climax and then
begins to diminish in intensity but is suddenly interrupted by a
fortissimo restatement of Exx. 1 and 4 in combination, at
measure 177, Ex. 4 again in stretto imitation. The passage
reaches its climax at measure 195, in which 6/8 triplets are
stated fortissimo by full orchestra. This tutti ostinato, based
upon the discord and rhythmic pattern that began the movement, gradually subsides to a held tone in high strings.

SECTION B (TRIO)

Measures 200-267. Against the sustained tone, a quiet
chord progression is slowly presented by the saxophone choir:

Ex. 5

etc.

Example 5, in 2/4, alternates with a rhythmic 6/8 pattern stressing duplets against triplets and employing glockenspiel, xylophone and pizzicato strings. After three such alternations, Ex. 5 is taken up by strings, flute and harp at measure 234, against an occasional obbligato of celesta and muted brass. Hemiola rhythmic juxtaposition is still prominent, and the texture is now highly contrapuntal. The passage gradually subsides to a brief silence.

SECTION A'

Measures 268-308. The silence is broken by a fortissimo restatement of Ex. 1 at measure 268, for full orchestra, in rhythmic augmentation and harmonized in parallel major triads. Example 1 resumes its initial form at measure 277, stated by the three saxophones, and is suddenly interrupted at measure 293 by the discordant rhythmic pattern of the movement's opening, out of which emerges the solo B-flat saxophone and side drum in a final fragment of Ex. 1. The side drum continues alone for a few measures and then dies away.

FOURTH MOVEMENT
(in two large sections)

PART I	repeated Binary form
Section A	measures 1-46
Section B	measures 47-62
Section A'	measures 63-87
Section B'	measures 88-117

Part II	Sonata-Allegro, plus Coda
Exposition	measures 118-166
Development	measures 167-190
Recapitulation	measures 191-219
Coda	measures 220-241

PART I—SECTION A

Measures 1-46. The movement opens with a slow, quiet passage for violins,

Ex. 1

which is imitated canonically by other strings and then by flute, clarinet and horn. The highly contrapuntal passage subsides upon a quiet harmonic figure, at measure 21, for brass, harp and pizzicato strings.

Ex. 2

Note the stress upon the semitone in Ex. 1 and the alternately raised and lowered inflection of the note D in Ex. 2. The quiet statement of Ex. 2 leads to a pianissimo pattern of woodwind figurations, punctuated by pizzicati strings. Against this ostinato, a lyric melody is presented by solo horn, beginning at measure 27:

Ex. 3

which is imitated canonically by other strings and then by

Example 3 is taken up by strings and flutes at measure 33,

against the continuing ostinato in winds and harp. A gradual crescendo begins, as the low winds and horns are added to the texture.

SECTION B

Measures 47-62. The crescendo builds to a restatement of Ex. 2 at measure 47, more elaborately scored, which rapidly diminishes to a pianissimo and leads directly to a new melodic figure at measure 53.

Ex. 4

In its ascending line and its rhythmic stresses, this motive bears some resemblance to Ex. 1 of the opening movement. Example 5 is stated at first by low strings and winds, then imitated canonically in the higher registers at measures 56 and 58. The passage subsides on a quiet harmonic progression that emphasizes the semitonal clash between the alternately major and minor third scale degree:

Ex. 5

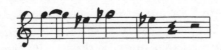

SECTION A'

Measures 63-87. Against a background of harp chords, the solo oboe states a variant of Ex. 1, beginning at measure 63, and other solo instruments are gradually added to the contrapuntal texture. A flute variant of Ex. 1, more elaborate and florid, appears at measure 72, imitated by solo violin at measure 77. Example 3 enters quietly at measure 78, in the low register against the florid string figurations. As the instrumentation grows richer, a gradual crescendo begins.

SECTION B'

Measures 88-117. The crescendo leads to a vigorous re-statement of Ex. 2 at measure 88, which in turn leads directly to a slow, forceful presentation of Ex. 4 at measure 97, imi-tated canonically and building to a fortissimo at measure 103. The passage subsides on a quiet stretto between horn and trumpet and an answering phrase for strings, both based upon Ex. 4.

PART II — EXPOSITION

Measures 118-166. There is a brief pause, interrupting an expected cadence, and the cadence is completed with a sus-tained high G at measure 118, punctuated by pizzicati strings. An extended melody appears in the violas at measure 120, under the sustained note G:

Ex. 6

Example 6 is extended and developed through contrapuntal imitation, as other strings are added to the texture, and then woodwinds at measure 134. A sudden crescendo leads to a more fully scored expansion of the triplet figure of Ex. 6 and to a forceful motive at measure 157, stated by high strings and winds and introduced by a crash of the cymbal and bass drum.

Ex. 7

Example 7 is imitated canonically at measure 158, and Ex. 4

is added to the contrapuntal texture at measure 162, in rhythmic augmentation.

DEVELOPMENT

Measures 167-190. At measure 167, a vigorous brass statement of Ex. 6 is added to the already heavy contrapuntal texture, and Ex. 4 in rhythmic augmentation again appears at measure 173 in the low register, taken up by the high winds, brasses and strings at measure 176. As Ex. 4 gains in prominence, its relation to Ex. 1 of the opening movement becomes apparent. The climax of the passage is interrupted by a restatement of Ex. 2, suddenly quiet, at measure 180, answered by the short motive of Ex. 5. A sudden crescendo leads to a fortissimo on Ex. 5 at measure 187, which grows in intensity.

RECAPITULATION

Measures 191-219. The crescendo is interrupted by an unexpectedly quiet restatement of Ex. 7 at measure 191, its initial figure repeated again and again in increasing crescendo. Example 4 is added to the texture at the height of this crescendo, beginning at measure 197, and Ex. 6 reappears at measure 202, in rhythmic augmentation and set in two-voice counterpoint for full orchestra. This march-like passage gradually subsides to a quiet statement of Ex. 5 in the low registers.

CODA

Measures 220-241. After a brief silence, Ex. 5 reappears fortissimo and scored for full orchestra, alternating with a figure of Ex. 4 and building to an E major chord at measure 232. Against this sustained chord, the saxophones present the "Neapolitan" motive of the opening movement (see movement I, Ex. 2). The F major chord is absorbed into the

E major, and the process repeated twice more before the E major triad is finally asserted alone, triple-forte, only to subside and very softly fade away to silence.

❖   ❖   ❖

It may be questionable whether or not a composer's age is a pertinent factor in the analysis of his music, but in this instance it seems inescapable. One must admit that the Vaughan Williams Ninth Symphony represents a unique achievement for a composer in his eighties. The significance of the composer's age rests not in the worth of the music *per se,* which is a matter of individual taste, but in its extraordinary youthfulness, its freshness of approach. In its form and orchestration, the Ninth Symphony reveals new interests and objectives on the part of its composer. In this sense, it is, like the *Sinfonia Antartica* and the Eighth Symphony, an experimental work.

There are, of course, many features of the work that are reminiscent of earlier Vaughan Williams symphonies. One is reminded of the enlarged percussion section of the *Sinfonia Antartica* and the Eighth Symphony, as well as of the saxophone of the Sixth Symphony. The flugelhorn solo recalls, perhaps, the natural horn and trumpet of the *Pastoral Symphony*. The dissonant counterpoint of the Scherzo is reminiscent of the Fourth Symphony and Sixth Symphony. The cyclic use of a pervasive motive and the finale that subdivides into smaller "movements" are to be observed in the early *A Sea Symphony*.

Yet in Dickinson's words, "here is no emulation of other ninth symphonies, but one more pleasant chant of exploration for those still young enough to launch out."[1] James Day, in a similar vein, adds that

Perhaps none of this (the musical material) is new — and yet it is a new rearrangement of elements which we have noted before in Vaughan Williams' music. . . . Even so late in life the veteran composer shows his ability to surprise. . . . It is the work, not of a tired old man, but of a very experienced one. . . .[2]

PART THREE

STRUCTURE, STYLE,
AND MEANING

Structural Considerations

With the exception of the *Sinfonia Antartica,* which has five movements, the symphonies are four-movement works. Each of the symphonies, however, is organized in a unique manner. With respect to both the order of movements and the internal structure of individual movements, not one of the symphonies duplicates any other.

FORM

If the standard order of movements is assumed to be *I.* Moderate speed, Sonata-Allegro form, *II.* Slow, *III.* Fast and light, *IV.* Moderate or fast, and weighty, then only five of the nine symphonies can be termed "conventional": the *Sea, London, Pastoral,* Fourth and Ninth. In the Fifth and Eighth Symphonies the usual order of slow movement and Scherzo is reversed, while the Finale of the Sixth Symphony is in effect the slow movement of the work. The *Sinfonia Antartica,* a five-movement work, has two slow movements, both of which occur after the Scherzo.

It should also be noted that the *Pastoral Symphony,* while outwardly conforming to the standard sequence, really produces the effect of three slow movements broken only by the contrasting lightness of the third movement Scherzo.

Opening movements. Five of the nine opening movements are organized along the principles of Sonata-Allegro form, although no two treat the form in exactly the same way. These differences are in no sense unusual; similar alterations will be found in Sonata-Allegro movements of any composer, including those of the classic Haydn, Mozart and Beethoven.

167

The Sonata-Allegro is traditionally not so much a set form as a broad plan of organization, one which stresses the resolution of contrasting elements. The differences in Vaughan Williams' treatment of various Sonata movements require no special comment, then, in this respect.

Four opening movements, however, are not in Sonata-Allegro form. The Sixth Symphony opens with a Sonatina movement, omitting a development section, although it has been maintained that the development occurs between the statements of the first and second theme groups.[1] The opening movement of the Fifth Symphony, a Sonatina, substitutes a lengthy transition for the traditional development section. The *Sinfonia Antartica* begins with a sectional movement in which the principle of repetition is abandoned in favor of the idea of growth from one motive to another. In the Eighth Symphony, the opening movement may appear to retain the logic of the Sonata-Allegro, but is in fact cast in the form of a set of Variations.

Slow movements. Note that the designation "slow" does not necessarily refer to the second movement of the work. For example, the slow movements of the fifth and eighth symphonies are the third movements.

These movements can be roughly divided into two categories: those that are either three-part song forms (ABA) or variants of that form, and those which are organized along completely different principles, either binary or sectional. The second group is represented by the slow movement of the F minor Symphony, a Sonata-Allegro, and the sectional Finale of the Sixth Symphony. The third movement (Cavatina) of the Eighth Symphony is also a binary Sonatina.

Simple three-part song forms (ABA) occur in the slow movements of the *Sea, London* and Sixth Symphonies.[2] The slow movement of the Fifth Symphony, while also ABA, treats the middle section as a development section, as does the "Intermezzo" of the *Sinfonia Antartica*. The form has been expanded into a song form with repeated Trio (ABAB) in the *Pastoral* and Ninth Symphonies and is a more symmetrical

ABCBA in the "Landscape" movement of the *Sinfonia Antartica.*

Scherzo movements. Note again that the term designates light rapid movements, but does not necessarily refer to third movements.

The three-part Scherzo and Trio form (ABA) is adhered to in four of the symphonies (the Fourth, *Sinfonia Antartica,* Eighth and Ninth) and has been expanded into a Scherzo with repeated Trio (ABABA) in the *Pastoral* and Sixth. A Scherzo with two Trios, akin to a Second Rondo form (ABACA), occurs in the *London* and Fifth Symphonies, while *A Sea Symphony* presents the only non-ternary Scherzo movement of the nine, a binary Sonatina.

Finales. The most extensively used form for the closing movement is the three-part song, ABA, which occurs in the *London,* Fifth and *Sinfonia Antartica.* It should be noted, however, that the Finale of the Fifth Symphony, although ternary in over-all outlines, is in fact a Passacaglia, or set of polyphonic variations on a melodic ground bass.

Both *A Sea Symphony* and the Ninth Symphony present long sectional Finales, which can in fact be divided into smaller complete "movements." The closing movements of the Fourth Symphony and *Pastoral Symphony* are in Sonata-Allegro form, while the Finale of the Eighth is a light Rondo.

The Epilogue. Vaughan Williams' greatest contribution to the development of the symphonic form is the unique concept of the "Epilogue." In one respect, the Epilogue is merely an extension of the earlier idea of a coda; that is, it can be thought of as 'the coda to the entire symphony. It also serves a much more important function, that of summarizing and clarifying the important ideas — musical and otherwise — of the work and bringing them to a focal point. In this respect, then, the Epilogue places the heaviest weight, the point of culmination, at the very end of the symphony and unites all the movements in a pattern of growth that extends from the beginning of the work to its conclusion. This concept of continuous growth, first made explicit by Beethoven, was further developed during the nineteenth century, and can be seen most clearly in the works of Brahms and Mahler.

In two of the symphonies — the *London* and the F minor — the Epilogue is a separate, fifth movement. In each of the other works the last movement proper serves as the Epilogue and is in fact designated as such by a title in the Sixth and *Sinfonia Antartica.*

Since the final movements, then, function as summaries, they contain references to musical material previously used in the work. These may be direct quotations, possibly altered by new context, as in the final pages of the *London,* Fourth, Fifth and *Sinfonia Antartica,* or more indirect references which contain the essence of previous material. This latter practice was also first made explicit by Beethoven. That is, we may assume that such themes as

serve as final commentaries upon earlier themes,

and are thus directly related to the previous material. In the
same sense, the opening of the Finale of *A Sea Symphony* is a
variant of that work's main motive.[3]

The Epilogue of the Sixth Symphony makes use of all the
important musical ideas of preceding movements, combined,
however, into a new theme.

Or, to use still another example, the main theme of the
Eighth Symphony's final Toccata movement makes use of
descending fourths, rather than the ascending fourths of the
work's opening measures.

MELODY

Vaughan Williams' style is essentially a melodic one, with its origins in vocal music. As Foss notes,

> not only with voices and verse has Vaughan Williams sought his melodic ideal, but also in forging a singing part for an instrument, in bringing a voice into his *Pastoral Symphony*, in making his viola and 'cello and other inner instruments play parts far more vocal and expressive than [other composers'] voice parts.[4]

Two distinct types of melodic writing occur frequently in the symphonies. One of these is modal and primarily pentatonic, thus utilizing patterns of fourths and fifths:

Melodies written in this style are often slow and contemplative, complex rhythmically (with much alternation of duplets and triplets) but not strong metrically. Some of them are, in fact, measureless. There is also a tendency towards melismatic ornamentation of single tones, a characteristic of early modal music such as Gregorian Chant.

Another characteristic of modal music is the flat seventh degree rather than the leading tone seventh which was present only in the Lydian (and later Ionian) mode. The flat seventh, which is quite common in Vaughan Williams' music, appeared early in his development as a composer. Both Stanford and Bruch complained of the idiosyncrasy.

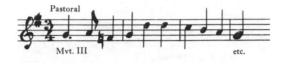

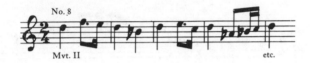

A second melodic tendency, while also modal, leans toward the more strictly diatonic major and minor. Melodies of this type are often strongly metric, with simpler "square-cut" rhythmic patterns, and again recall characteristics of English folk song.

Chromaticism, not native to the style, is introduced consciously as a foreign element for dramatic and expressive purposes.[5] Chromatic tones are used either in connection with isolated intervals (usually the semitone or the augmented fourth) which acquire structural and emotional significance through repetition:

or through the alternately major and minor inflections of important intervals in a melodic line. This latter practice bears a strong resemblance to the technique of cross relations, a stylistic feature of early English music.[6]

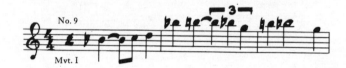

Neither of these chromatic techniques can be associated with the twelve-tone tonal system of Wagner or the chromatically atonal practices of Schönberg. Vaughan Williams' chromaticism is not a natural, spontaneous means of expression, as was Wagner's, but a way of *heightening* expression when placed within the context of a diatonic, modal, often pentatonic, style.

HARMONY

Chords are often used for their sensual, coloristic effects, rather than in series of root movements which drive toward a cadence. These chord sequences are composed of harmonies of a single color, usually triads in first or second inversion, which are set under the melodic line and follow its contours.[7]

This technique of Vaughan Williams has two main sources: the composer's study with Ravel and absorption of impressionistic idioms, and his interest in early English music, which deals extensively in parallel thirds and sixths.

Since harmonies are built from the melody downwards rather than from the bass up, chord color takes precedence over root progression. Root progressions and cadential effects do exist, however. They differ from those of traditional harmony in one simple respect: they are compatible with modal melody rather than with the major-minor system of the past two centuries. For example, a pair of major triads whose roots move from 7(lowered)-8 of the scale forms a convincing modal cadence. This may also be a progression of three major triads, whose roots move out from 6(lowered)-7 (lowered)-8.

The evaded or deceptive cadence is also possible within a modal context. In the two examples following, the lowered 7

triad (which functions in the modal cadence above) is also the dominant of a *major key* a minor third above the modal "final." As in the examples below, an excursion into this major key prolongs the eventual cadence into the more important (modal) tonality. Also note that in both examples the secondary (major) tonality is emphasized by means of a plagal cadence, or IV-I relation.

There is a tendency towards alternation of major and minor triads. These may be related through a common tone,

or unrelated.

They may occur in the course of traditional root movement,

or as alternating members of a parallel chord series.

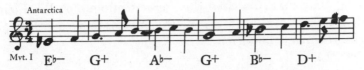

Mvt. I   Eb−   G+   Ab−   G+   Bb−   D+

The juxtaposition of major and minor triads, like the use of chromatic melody, is often reserved for passages of great dramatic import and seems to have a highly expressive meaning for Vaughan Williams.

It should be noted, finally, that the frequency of triadic writing does not, in this case, imply strongly tonal leanings. Tonality is obscured, rather, through the devices cited above. In addition, there are instances of harmonies built on roots which move in whole tones and other non-tonal patterns.

All twelve chromatic tones are thus at the composer's disposal, although used in a triadic, diatonic context. Vaughan Williams, like Purcell, "has discovered how to combine folk-song colour with chromatic harmony. This seems to be the secret of his creative gift: that he does not sacrifice progress to tradition, or tradition to progress."[8]

COUNTERPOINT

Since Vaughan Williams' main interest is in melody, his textures are primarily contrapuntal rather than harmonic. It is in this area that he differs most radically from his great contemporary symphonist and folklorist, Sibelius.

The symphonies not only make use of contrapuntal forms,
among which may be cited the fugue-Epilogue of the Fourth
and the Passacaglia of the Fifth, but contain countless passages featuring imitation.

Examples of fugato and ground-bass occur frequently.
Overlapping stretto imitation is used extensively as well.

Ostinato patterns are often employed in all the symphonies.
These may take the form of simple pedal points,

complex figurations,

or repeated series of chords, set in distinctive rhythmic patterns. The "oom-pah" bass, which is one of these, represents a sardonic vein in the composer's style. In fact, it has been said to show "Vaughan Williams parodying Vaughan Williams."[9]

An interesting device, introduced in the *Pastoral Symphony* and used infrequently in subsequent works, consists of the polyphonic combination of melodic lines, *each* accompanied by its own series of parallel triadic harmonies (see Harmony).

This results in an effect of polychordal blocks moving simultaneously in different planes.

RHYTHM, METER, TEMPO

As mentioned previously, one characteristic of Vaughan Williams' style is slow but rhythmically complex melody, dealing mainly in combinations of duplets and triplets. Meter, on the other hand, is not strongly emphasized in such melodies, and a few of them are actually notated without bar lines.

When such melodies are combined contrapuntally, the effect is a continual interweaving of duplets and triplets, or simultaneous two-against-three patterns.

The hemiola, a similar effect, occurs frequently throughout the symphonies. The unit of an entire measure, rather than a single beat, is alternately (or simultaneously) divided into two and three pulses.

The relaxed attitude toward meter is also evident in all of Vaughan Williams' writing, except that which is directly evocative of folk dance. Even many passages which are strongly metrical do not adhere to the *written* bar line. Rhythmic patterns occur within and across the bar line.

Changing meter is frequent.

The above rhythmic and metrical characteristics may be traced to Vaughan Williams' great interest in vocal melody, in song rather than in dance. Much of his music flows evenly, but according to the narrative patterns of human speech rather than the balanced symmetry of poetry and stylized dance patterns.

Changes of tempo occur frequently within movements and serve to define the form, thus outlining the main divisions within movements. Finally, all three time factors — rhythm, meter and tempo — are extensively employed in the transformation and development of themes, either within a movement or from one movement to the next.

ORCHESTRATION

A string player himself, Vaughan Williams uses the string body of the orchestra quite effectively. There are numerous passages for divided strings, muted strings, and solo violin, viola or 'cello parts dominating the rest of the string ensemble.

The composer's fondness for the strings has been noted by commentators. Payne claims that Vaughan Williams' concern with vocal melody is directly related to his use of the strings, for "string tone (next to vocal tone) is most indicative of human feelings."[10]

Vaughan Williams' orchestration is basically conservative and traditional. Young notes that the orchestration of the symphonies is "not virtuoso," and suggests that this indicates the composer's "lack of passionate intensity in so far as physical values are concerned."[11] One may feel, in fact, that the Vaughan Williams orchestra is used most effectively for purposes of *understatement;* for example, full tuttis or extensive mixing of colors occur only rarely. Vaughan Williams tends to separate orchestral forces into distinct families or choirs, rather than to create complex color mixtures, i.e. colors resulting from doubling instruments in different families. This is a technique derived from French impressionism, one which the composer most probably learned through his study with Ravel.

Doubling *per se* is generally avoided, and solo passages are prominently featured throughout the symphonies. Young, in noting the lack of "unnecessary duplication," states that "each player feels his individual importance, while the musical proposition comes to the listener less ambiguously."[12] Doubling is not entirely absent, of course, and occurs at moments of great climax and fortissimo tutti passages. Concern with novel color mixtures is, nevertheless, not an essential factor in Vaughan Williams' style. There is little of the ceaseless searching for effects, the expansion of instrumental range, or the uncovering of new sounds on traditional instruments, which characterize much of contemporary orchestration. The instruments are, generally, used in their most characteristic registers, in a vocal rather than a virtuoso instrumental style.

Due to the strong emphasis upon melodic and contrapuntal textures, solo woodwind writing is frequent. This results in a light, open texture that emphasizes the interplay of contrasting colors and reveals the composer's strong attachment and deep indebtedness to a stylistic heritage basically *vocal* in nature. A concern with soloistic passages led Vaughan Williams to the use of instruments not common to the orchestra, such as the "natural" horn and trumpet, the human voice, saxophone, organ, tuned percussion and flugelhorn. In contrast to the passages employing pure solo colors, as noted above, climaxes and other dramatic moments are richly scored with much doubling. Tutti passages in only one or two parts (doubled in octaves) are frequent.

The harp is standard in Vaughan Williams' orchestra. It is rarely used in a lush, sweeping, romantic manner. Rather, it functions as a simple harmonic background, perhaps reminiscent of the plucked instruments which accompanied early English songs.

TONALITY

Clearly defined tonalities are difficult to distinguish in much of this music. Modality, modal counterpoint, and harmonies which do not involve standard root movement, all contribute to the difficulty. With Vaughan Williams, in Young's words, "classic tonality is in the melting pot. . . . F minor is epigrammatic for 'nearer F minor than any other old-fashioned key with which you may be acquainted. . . .' "[13]

Paradoxically, there is always a sense of *key*, or tonal center. The precise location of the tonal center is, however, often ambiguous. The composer himself was not sure whether the first movement of the Fifth Symphony was in G or D,[14] and the resolution of the problem is reserved for the final movement of the work. This difficulty is due to the initial ambiguity of using simple triads and seventh chords — the common speech of composers of the preceding two centuries, and used with diatonic major and minor implications — in a modal context. Another source of the problem is the use of all twelve chromatic tones in the triadic harmonization of diatonic melody.

Modulation is usually effected without elaborate preparation and resolution; this has been referred to as "modulation without tears."[15] Most modulations involve movement to the tonality of the mediant or submediant (major or minor). Modulation to the dominant or subdominant would seem to be too directly diatonic, and would thus dissipate the modal implications of the music. Similarly, modulations to more remote keys would seem too chromatic within the style.

In determining the key relationships of the various movements of a symphony, Vaughan Williams has — perhaps consciously, perhaps not — revealed an association between the large key areas and the important motive (or the combined intervals of several such motives) of the symphony. This does not occur in the case of all the symphonies, and in any event it is not a device that originates with Vaughan Williams; it is, however, an interesting and provocative example of the composer's debt to the nineteenth century concept of the cyclic symphony. These specific instances may illustrate this point more thoroughly: 1) the main tonalities of the four movements of *A Sea Symphony*, D, E, G, E-flat, spell a variant of motive B of that work; 2) the four main keys of *A London Symphony*, G, C, D, G, outline the main motive of the symphony; 3) the four movements of the Sixth Symphony are joined by semitones and augmented fourths, important intervals in the work as a whole. The semitonal conflict of the opening pages (E versus F) is pitched a minor second lower at the conclusion of the work (E-flat versus E-natural), and perhaps adds to the sense of resignation in the movement.

More distant relationships, although tenable ones, exist within the key structure of the *Sinfonia Antartica* and the Ninth Symphony.

Sources and Evolution of the Style

Two DISTINCT AND SOMEWHAT CONTRADICTORY influences shaped Vaughan Williams' symphonic style. One of these was the then newly discovered heritage of English music, both folk music and the art music from Dunstable to Purcell. The other was the great body of music that comprised the literature of the European Symphony, from Haydn to Brahms, Bruckner and Mahler.

The English influence was most valuable in determining many of the *details* of Vaughan Williams' musical language — the inclination towards modality, speech-rhythms, simple triads, and cross relations. It is probably this aspect of the composer's style that Foss refers to when he remarks,

With slight exceptions, the music of the nineteenth century composers seems to have passed him by, and, indeed, the music of most of the eighteenth century composers too. His genealogical line springs from the Tudor school and English folk-song; there is an intermarriage with Bach, but other composers are . . . not of the family circle.[1]

THE INFLUENCE OF FOLK SONG

It will be recalled that Vaughan Williams, early in his career, spent many years in the study of English folk song and English church music. His first teachers, Parry and Stanford, were among the pioneers in the revival of the English national style. And Max Bruch, while not English, was equally convinced of the value of native folk music for every composer. The results of this period of study are evident in Vaughan Williams' music and in his musical philosophy. As Foss states, "Vaughan Williams is influenced by English folk song just as Bach was influenced by the Lutheran Chorale."[2]

The comparison with J. S. Bach is worthy of further comment here; Vaughan Williams himself felt a strong affinity with Bach and his music. Like Bach, he felt himself to be an honest, practical musician rather than an avant-garde "composer." Like Bach, he had been thoroughly grounded in the folk music and art music of his countrymen. And, again like Bach, he directed his creative energies towards the moral and spiritual aspirations of his people. In these respects, Vaughan Williams' comments about Bach are particularly revealing: "The beauty of his music abides because his music appeals to everyone — not only to the aesthete, the musicologist or the propagandist, but above all to Whitman's 'Divine Average' — that great middle class from whom nearly all that is worthwhile in religion, painting, poetry and music has sprung."[3]

One influence of folk song upon Vaughan Williams' style has already been noted, namely the emphasis upon melody. This results in a vocal approach even in his instrumental music. Two other important stylistic factors derive from the folk song influence. One of these is the association of music with speech and hence with "meaning"; in Dickinson's terms, this results in music that contains "matter as well as manner." The second factor is the tendency to avoid overstatement. "The folk-singer is not in the vulgar sense a public entertainer . . . when he has had his say, he departs quietly."[4] Much of Vaughan Williams' music is similarly concise; it concentrates on essentials. Almost all his movements end softly, on a fading pianissimo.

Folk song has affected Vaughan Williams' melodic style in many ways. The pentatonic and modal character of his writing is one of these — much of his thematic material is pentatonic, modal, or both. Another important effect is the use of the whole tone, not only at cadences but in much harmonic root movement and in the melisma of his melodic lines. When these linear elements are combined contrapuntally, they result in modal polyphony, or novel "vertical" effects which may be termed polychords.

These influences are most obviously felt in the *Pastoral Symphony,* which is almost exclusively melodic in texture, rhythmically complex and metrically free, built on pentatonic, modal and whole-tone patterns and figurations. The symphony is simple, concise, a masterpiece of understatement in which every movement ends by vanishing into silence. Holst, who knew both Vaughan Williams and the English tradition very well, writing of the *Pastoral Symphony* in a letter to its composer in 1933, declared, "It's the very essence of you."[5]

THE EUROPEAN TRADITION

On the other hand, the influence of the European symphonic tradition was important in the shaping of the larger aspects of Vaughan Williams' symphonic style, his approach to the symphony as a form and as an artistic means of expression. It would therefore be a mistake to think of Vaughan Williams as exclusively English in a narrow, insular sense. European music contributed heavily to the formulation of his musical philosophy and style; as Ottaway points out, Vaughan Williams began his career in the vein of the late nineteenth century European nationalists, absorbed many techniques of the French impressionists, and at his maturity was recognized as a European humanist.[6]

The European symphonic tradition of the eighteenth and nineteenth centuries has been more widely discussed and written about than any other great body of musical literature. It seems sufficient, therefore, to state that Vaughan Williams did not depart from this tradition. His sole formal innovation, the Epilogue, is the logical extension of a tendency existent in the nineteenth century — in fact, it derives naturally from the dramatic plan implicit in Beethoven, the wish to reach the highest dramatic point, the summation and culmination, at the very end of the work. Vaughan Williams, rather than breaking with the symphonic tradition, drew heavily upon it in many ways.

In each of the symphonies, thematic material is quoted,

developed and transformed from one movement to the next, thus unifying all the movements. This practice originated with Beethoven, and can be found in the works of Franck, D'Indy, Schumann, Brahms and Tchaikovsky. There is a tendency to alter the usual order or number of movements. This tendency, which may also be traced to Beethoven, appears in much of the romantic symphonic literature — Berlioz, Liszt, Franck, Saint-Saëns and Tchaikovsky, among others. In each symphony, the final movement is the climactic point of the work, a summation of main ideas of the entire symphony. This concept of the Epilogue is derived from a romantic tendency that began with Beethoven and Berlioz and is highly characteristic of Brahms, Bruckner and Mahler.

Four of the symphonies are explicitly programmatic: the *Sea, London, Pastoral* and *Sinfonia Antartica.* The influence of the program symphony — which appears as early as Haydn and occurs in the music of Beethoven, Berlioz, Mendelssohn, Schumann and others — and of the symphonic poem cannot be doubted. The introduction of the human voice into the symphonic texture, which begins with the Beethoven Ninth Symphony, can be found in the works of Liszt, Mahler and Debussy. Three of Vaughan Williams' symphonies — the *Sea, Pastoral* and *Sinfonia Antartica* — are also choral or vocal in part. This tendency, however, is not exclusively derived from the European models. It is much more likely that Vaughan Williams' works for voice(s) and orchestra, like Holst's, were influenced by the English musical tradition, which is primarily vocal and choral.

EVOLUTION OF THE STYLE

The dates of the symphonies span a period of almost half a century. During this time, each new work that appeared, while unmistakably "Vaughan Williams," presented some radical departure from the style or mood of its predecessors. In retrospect, all the symphonies are stylistically consistent, making use of the techniques discussed previously. Each of them, nevertheless, differs from the others in mood and emotional content.

This apparent contradiction has resulted in conflicting opinions of the works and the composer. It has been said that Vaughan Williams is guilty of employing mannerisms — that all of his works have the same stylistic idiosyncrasies and sound the same.[7] It has also been claimed that, on the contrary, Vaughan Williams' nine symphonies have a greater range of variety than Beethoven's nine, Brahms's four or Sibelius' seven.[8]

Both statements are true in part. Although each work presents purely musical, stylistic changes, these are introduced slowly and gradually. The musical language and the total sound impression of the last symphony of 1957 are not unlike those of the first symphony of 1910. New elements have been added and new emphases discovered, but the style is essentially the same. The change in attitude, in expressive ends and means, is much more striking. As Foss states, each symphony is meant "to serve a different human purpose."[9]

The first three symphonies are obviously programmatic, although the tendency towards a specific program is lessened with each succeeding work. All three bear descriptive titles; *A Sea Symphony* is explicit in the use of a text, however, while the *London* is much more general in its references, the quotations and sound effects notwithstanding. The *Pastoral Symphony* is the least specific of the three, and evokes no pictorial-literary images of any kind. It is impressionistic in the purest sense of the term.

The middle three symphonies, continuing this tendency, have completely submerged their programs in favor of a more absolute but equally *dramatic* approach. Descriptive titles are abandoned, and the symphonies are designated by key. They are, however, vitally concerned with subject matter. Each deals with a state of mind, perhaps the state of Europe, and either of these states is a more complex stimulus than the sea, the city or the countryside.

Anyone who has lived through the second quarter of this

century will understand these symphonies as a series of reactions to contemporary events — the Fourth as a chronicle
of Fascism and an unwitting prediction of war, the Fifth a
consoling vision of the peace, and the Sixth a bitter disillusionment with that peace. Future generations will not react to the
symphonies in this way, but the works are so unified and well
organized as absolute music that they should not suffer
thereby. The same cannot be honestly said for the first three
symphonies, which lose effectiveness if the references are not
grasped.

It is this ideal fusion of the dramatic and the "absolute"
which mark these middle three symphonies as truly great
works, equal to the finest symphonies of the past. They are
neither entertaining collages of abstract patterns nor stories
set to music, but works with a sense of unity, purpose and
conviction. They are narrative but never literal. That is, in
this writer's judgment, the essence of symphony, and the best
symphonies of all periods and styles possess it.

With the last three symphonies, Vaughan Williams' approach has become even more absolute, thus following the
single trend to its conclusion. Even the *Sinfonia Antartica,*
ostensibly programmatic and bearing textual references, is
conceived of as a suite of contrasting movements. The whole
is balanced but not unified, even though a literal content is
provided. The Eighth and Ninth Symphonies are similarly
lightweight, concerned more with contrast and balance than
with unity and direction. The cyclic form of the Ninth, and
its heavy finale, attempt to compensate for this, but cannot.

This weakening of content would seem to imply a deteriora-
tion of the composer's creative powers in his aging years, but
it actually indicates a shift of emphasis and experimentation
in a new field of interest, that of orchestration and sonority
per se. In Vaughan Williams' last years, such works as the
Concerto for Tuba and Orchestra and the *Romance* for Harmonica and Strings appeared. This preoccupation with novel
instrumental combinations is apparent in the last symphonies
as well. The *Sinfonia Antartica* makes use of organ, wind

machine and extensive percussion. The four movements of the Eighth Symphony are organized about different ensembles (including tuned percussion), and the flugelhorn and saxophone choir appear in the Ninth Symphony.

Among other tendencies that may be observed during the course of Vaughan Williams' symphonic career, the increasing use of melodic and contrapuntal textures is most notable. Beginning with the *Pastoral Symphony,* ground bass, fugato, canonic imitation and sustained ostinati become more frequent. Concurrent with this increased emphasis upon counterpoint, and very possibly related to it, is a growing interest in orchestral color, particularly in the combinations of solo instruments. Vaughan Williams himself admits to overscoring in his early works, and speaks of his later restraint in orchestration.[10]

Chromaticism, while always present in the composer's style (see Melody, Harmony and Tonality), takes on great dramatic implications in the Fourth Symphony and functions as a highly expressive force in subsequent works. Melodically, the intervals of the semitone and augmented fourth are used to portray violence or an insidious, evil quality. Another melodic device, the alternately major and minor inflection of an important thematic interval, is more sardonic in its implications. Very often coupled with an "oom-pah" or other ostinato figure, it expresses irony or parody. Harmonically, the alternation of major and minor triads becomes increasingly more pronounced throughout the symphonies and serves a variety of expressive needs, dependent upon such factors as tempo, scoring, and dynamics.

The Problem of Meaning

THE PROBLEM OF CONTENT in music is one that plagues analysts and critics of music, and students and teachers in appreciation courses. The layman's initial response to music is often one of association: the expressive qualities of the music are linked with similarly evocative extramusical stimuli. Thus the misconception originates that all music bears a specific content that can be translated into verbal or visual terms. The composer, in other words, "tells a story" or "paints a picture," and music as a self-sufficient, autonomous means of expression is all but ignored. Educators and commentators have attempted to combat this impression by drawing a line between two distinct types of music: "program" music and "abstract" music. The former has an explicit subject or story, while the latter is expressive in and of *itself*. Moreover, the meaning of an "abstract"work is to be found in its purely musical structure, its themes and their manipulations, texture, patterns and general architectural design. These structural features, when recognized and understood, actually do take on a meaning, in the sense that the direction, continuity and plan of the work become apparent. The listener can comprehend a piece as a unit, rather than as a loosely organized succession of sounds.

It is impossible, however, to convince the listener that a work has no other meaning than its structure. He continues to respond to the emotional power of music, including "abstract" music. Even though he has accepted the intrinsically musical nature of the expression and rejected any extramusical connotations, the very existence of expression is a fact that he cannot deny. And, as the argument runs, if music is expressive at all, it is expressive of *something* — something which is not merely inferred by the listener, but intended by the composer. In Ernest Newman's words, "A composer's imagination functions not as a self-contained faculty on a sort of desert island of its own, but as a whole; the whole man thinks."[1] Or, as Cardus states,

Obviously it is absurd to listen to [a composer's work] as an "objective pattern" and to attend to him as if he were a sort of monstrous spider spinning a web of tone by instinct. Music is no more "abstract" than poetry; it is a language in and through which composers have expressed themselves, their conceptions and visions of the world, precisely as Shakespeare, Goethe, Dante, Cervantes and Lewis Carroll have expressed theirs.[2]

Thus much music must be thought of being both abstract and yet meaningful. This apparent paradox is most evident in the Sonata forms — the sonata, quartet, concerto and symphony. The Sonata-Allegro, or first movement form, employs contrasts of tonalities, themes or moods, and eventually resolves these contrasts. It is, therefore, constructed of the two elements common to all musical forms: unity and variety. In the less complex part forms, i.e. ABA, Minuet or Scherzo-and-Trio, or Rondo, variety is interjected among unified, recurring elements, while the variation form involves the initial statement of a complete idea (unity) and its subsequent alteration (variety). The peculiar nature of the Sonata-Allegro, however, involves the resolution of contrasts, i.e. growth from the incomplete to the complete, from variety to unity. This principle of conflict and its resolution, plus the close relationship between early symphony and the opera, would tend to place the sonata or symphony within a tradition of dramatic music, although nonetheless "abstract."

After Beethoven, the principle of growth from the incomplete to the complete, the predominating feature of the first movement form, extends throughout all the movements of the sonata or symphony. H. C. Colles, in writing of the Romantic symphony, states that

Symphony is organic music. . . . All that is essential to a symphonic character is that the initial motive should in its inception represent to the composer's mind some issue larger than itself, and the subsequent movement or group of movements must reveal to the hearer what that larger issue is.[3]

It could even be claimed that the only truly abstract music in our literature is the instrumental music of the Baroque, the concertos, fugues, suites and passacaglias that precede the birth of the Sonata. Dickinson writes,

It is futile to *insist* that a symphony shall be a chain of sonorities, pure and simple . . . the "Sinfonia" began as an operatic overture, in contact with real life at one remove. . . . Beethoven . . . drew freely from his experience outside music for some of his symphonies. . . . A composer may write music for the mere interest of its relationships, or for their revealing associations. The listener who will not take the trouble to use more than his ears is just denying his birthright as an intelligent being . . . he is in danger of rejecting music which cannot be heard as sheer sonority.[4]

Few listeners can hope to miss the implications of meaning in the symphonies of Ralph Vaughan Williams. As Howells notes, "each of his major compositions has power to relate itself to some aspect, cause, or aspiration of contemporary life."[5] Although dramatic emphasis is implicit in the symphonic form itself, Vaughan Williams' predisposition towards vocal and choral music results in a strong sense of the narrative. While not programmatic, much of his abstract music is so intense as to border on the theatrical.

A large part of his originality can be traced to its origin in the composer's natural power of song, and his approach to music through the voice — with the odd duality, almost paradoxical, which this means; for song is at once the most personal and essentially musical method of musical expression, and yet by its nature it relies on the extra-musical expressive means of words.[6]

Much of the composer's rhythmic structure, e.g. the interweaving of duplets and triplets, can be traced to his experience in the setting of the English language, as well as his knowledge of folk song and its rhythmic subtleties. His polyphonic part writing is also influenced by his considerable amount of experience in the setting of choral music.

His vocabulary of expressive symbols is limited, as is the music's meaning. Vaughan Williams expressed himself in clear, direct, often blunt ways, in his written English as well as his musical speech. His choice of subject matter, in both music and essays, is limited to the more important issues in which he can clearly define his terms and simply state his case. The monumental scale of his symphonic subject matter and the unequivocal stand which he takes are both indicative of a moralistic outlook. Vaughan Williams' affinity with such literary figures as Bunyan and Whitman reflects this outlook as well. Perhaps for these reasons, he has been compared to the Biblical prophets;[7] if a less extravagant analogy is called for, his directness and boldness of manner can be compared to that of Beethoven.

His musical language is equally clear and direct. The norm is diatonic, often pentatonic, limited in melodic range and smooth in melodic contour, expressive of contemplation. Deviations from this norm represent external intrusions upon this state of peace: more jagged rhythms, often polyrhythms and hemiola, an expansion of the melodic range to its extremes, sharply defined meter, incessant ostinati such as the "oom-pah," and, particularly, chromaticism in melodic line and chord sequence. These may express moods of irony, terror, or simply great activity of a lighter nature. In all his moods, Vaughan Williams seems to proceed on the level of narrative, perhaps in accordance with his expressed belief that music has its origins in impassioned and intensified speech.[8]

If this is so, the symphonies are indeed abstract drama. They employ the inflections of speech rather than the specific references of speech, the expressive punctuation rather than the actual content. This is perhaps the prime function of music: to render in precise terms those aspects of language, i.e. pitch, duration and volume intensity, which the written word, with its precise meaning, leaves indeterminate.

EPILOGUE

A Critique of the Symphonies

IN HIS NINE SYMPHONIES, Ralph Vaughan Williams made major contributions both to English music and to symphonic literature. Although the two are interrelated, individually each marks a significant achievement in this century.

By a fortunate coincidence, Vaughan Williams' early musical training occurred at the point in history when England became conscious of her musical past. He was thus directed, through many sources, to a study of English folk music and art music; in the course of this study, he became aware of the existence of a national style that had once flourished but had died with Purcell.

It is to his credit that, through his efforts and those of Gustave Holst, this style was revived and incorporated into the serious English music of this century. It was shown to be compatible with the large forms developed in Europe during the preceding two hundred years, and even infused these forms with new life.

Much of Vaughan Williams' pioneering in the fusion of an indigenous English manner with the European symphony could and should have been accomplished during the eighteenth and nineteenth centuries. His major achievement, in effect, was to bring England back into the mainstream of musical composition. English composers of later generations, such as Walton, Rubbra and Britten, who carried this fusion further, produced the mature works that can only develop in a nation with a symphonic tradition. Vaughan Williams, almost singlehandedly, gave England this tradition.

"Tradition" is, although precise, perhaps an unfortunate word to use with reference to Vaughan Williams. He not

199

only returned to England her musical tradition but himself *became* a tradition in his own lifetime. To the British, Vaughan Williams was indeed a "Master" in every sense, and perhaps understandably so. Through his labors in editing and arranging native music as well as in composing, he made his name widely known to his countrymen. As a good craftsman of the *Gebrauchsmusik* persuasion, he wrote many works directly intended for a functional role in the ritual life of his country: music for church services, choir festivals, holidays, pageants, the schools. It is not difficult, then, to comprehend the purely national tendencies in Vaughan Williams' career which endeared him to his countrymen.

Such great esteem may have its drawbacks, and in Vaughan Williams' case, his association with the English tradition and his own position as a living tradition helped to further the notion that he was a traditional composer. When any public figure is regarded as a national monument by his own contemporaries, as Vaughan Williams was, in some strange way he ceases to be a contemporary himself. His work ceases to provoke, anger, excite or mystify — it exerts no direct force upon contemporary developments. And so, less than a decade since his death, Ralph Vaughan Williams is remembered by most as a figure of the early, remote years of this century — a contemporary not of Schönberg and Stravinsky but of Sibelius and Strauss. Like the latter two, he was often referred to as a classic in his own lifetime — a tactful, well-meaning but patronizing admission that, to many of his listeners, he was a living anachronism. Perhaps these are, then, the inevitable consequences of being so intimately associated with tradition.

The label "traditional" is, in fact, unfair to Vaughan Williams' chief virtue, his amazing flexibility and willingness to incorporate new resources into his work. Unlike Sibelius and Strauss, he did not terminate his artistic career in the 1920's, spending his last years in a state of relative unproductivity. On the contrary, he continued his creative work until the end

of his life, unfailingly maturing as an artist until the last. The
musical advances of the 1940's and 1950's were not lost on
him; he produced in these years works that reveal new interests, a fresh approach to problems of timbre, dissonance,
tonality, and musical form. Although the Post-Webern school
of serial composers regarded (and some continue to regard)
Vaughan Williams as the arch-conservative, other composers
of our time — equally "avant-garde," including proponents of
chance music, Third Stream and others quite unlike Vaughan
Williams stylistically — are beginning to discover the admi-
rable qualities that this man possessed: the sure trust in his
own musical instincts, the economy of means, the unwillingness
to follow the fad, the uncanny ability to impose his own personality upon the common language.

It is this last quality that sets him apart and will assure
him a place in the history of music. He managed to develop,
within the context of the traditional, a style that was unique
— and that was by all means *contemporary*. His music, in its
honest, direct way, expresses the tensions and contradictions
of this amazing century. This ability to express, to communi-
cate a feeling of emotional involvement, often an emotional
urgency, enabled him to master the abstract-dramatic form of
the symphony. Therein lies his second major achievement as a
composer.

❖   ❖   ❖

It may be said with truth that Vaughan Williams, Sibelius
and Prokofieff are the symphonists of this century. Their
efforts in this form are not only major contributions *per se,*
but continue the evolution of the symphony into the present
day. Vaughan Williams' particular contributions to the symphonic form are threefold. He expanded the traditional
tonal (i.e. major, minor) and harmonic approach to include
modality and polyphony as well. Secondly, his innovation of
the Epilogue serves to bind the individual movements of a
work into a single unit, a convincing means of reinforcing a

nineteenth century trend. Thirdly, he continued the tradition of abstract symphonic drama in a period which stressed the opposing poles of theatre music (ballet, opera, songs) and the austere Neo-Classic school — yet a period whose tensions and conflicts demanded musical expression, in purely musical terms.

Finally, his music acts as a constant reminder that originality may be achieved with a minimum of novelty and that the musical materials of the past are still adaptable for use in a thoroughly contemporary way by and for our own era.

APPENDIXES

Educational Implications

THE FOLLOWING NOTES ARE ADDRESSED primarily to teachers and students of music — not with the purpose of being prescriptive, offering specific curricula, or even introducing "music education" into a volume that, until now, has not dealt with this area. It is certain, however, that an intensive study of the symphonies of Ralph Vaughan Williams inevitably suggests certain problems that can be related to or utilized in the classroom.

THE TEACHING OF HARMONY AND COUNTERPOINT

The typical theory sequence, exclusive of courses in analysis and composition, consists of one year of diatonic harmony, one year of chromatic harmony, and one year of counterpoint in both sixteenth and eighteenth century styles. While this sequence of courses, as offered in most colleges, serves admirably to introduce the student to the stylistic features of the musical past, it leaves him unprepared to deal with contemporary idioms. But it is precisely in the area of contemporary music that the student needs increased understanding of compositional devices. This is essential in the training of the young composer and performer, since each is denied the alternative of tradition or common practice (always present when studying earlier music) upon which to base the practice of his own craft. The result of neglecting contemporary techniques is a widespread misunderstanding of modern music, compounded of fear and ignorance. The situation is particularly depressing because, for the most part, students (and the general public) are so saturated with the musical idiom of the nineteenth century that they have developed a conditioned response to that idiom and little else. Theory instruction, reflecting musical practice, usually stops with the idiom of the late nineteenth century, excepting the few class hours devoted to superficial speculation about contemporary techniques.

Teaching contemporary musical techniques on a more advanced level in such courses as analysis and composition may solve the problem in part, but it is overly restrictive. It narrows the application of the material to the specific area of analysis or composition. The resources of the twentieth century, like those of earlier periods, need to be related to every aspect of music-making: analysis, composition, dictation, singing, and keyboard application. That is, musical understanding, with respect to any style or period, must be integrated rather than isolated in approach. The ideal situation for such an approach is in the required theory sequence, not in advanced elective courses.

Of all twentieth century stylistic elements, the use of modes is perhaps easiest to introduce. It is directly related to the modal idioms of the Medieval and Renaissance periods, idioms studied in counterpoint classes. A comparative study of modality as used in these various periods would be quite useful. Modality should be presented initially in the study of harmony, if only to counteract the impression that modes lend themselves to contrapuntal rather than to harmonic treatment. Examples drawn from the music of Vaughan Williams are quite helpful in this respect. Such examples, as well as those drawn from folk song, demonstrate that modal melodies may be harmonized in a way that does not disturb the unique quality of the modal structure. At least one harmony textbook has dealt with the Aeolian mode, or natural minor scale, in this manner.[1] The approach can easily be extended to all other modes, the harmonic resources of which are consistently utilized by contemporary composers.[2]

It would be equally useful to introduce the study of contemporary modal polyphony in a course on sixteenth century counterpoint. Certain comparisons would quickly present themselves: while the examples drawn from both eras make use of the medieval modes, the later music exhibits greater freedom in rhythmic pattern, preparation and resolution of dissonance, and voice leading. Contemporary modal music, moreover, cannot fully disguise its heritage of two centuries in which diatonic, tonal, harmonic factors predominated. The cadences may be more pronounced and final in effect, and in many instances all twelve chromatic tones will be used within the modal context, through modulation to a different key center (while preserving the mode) or modulation from one mode to another.[3] Differences will be noted, however, that arise from the disparity of performance media: the early music is primarily vocal, whereas much of the contemporary music capitalizes on the wide ranges, leaps, skips and figurations possible with modern instruments.

The style of Vaughan Williams, therefore, is accessible to the beginner in that it is highly modal. Moreover, it deals basically with diatonic triads and seventh chords, material which has already been studied in harmony class. The difference in usage of this basic material, such as parallel chord series or unusual root progressions, provides excellent illustrations of the employment of traditional materials in fresh, distinctive ways.[4]

The use of contemporary music in theory classes can also be extended to the study of form, which is included in many integrated programs.

Various movements of the Vaughan Williams symphonies may be used to illustrate the many possible approaches to Sonata-Allegro form, the use of fugue and passacaglia in large-scale movements, and contemporary variants of the simple three-part Scherzo-and-Trio and Aria forms. Changes in the order of movements within a symphony can also be discussed.

All this has as its purpose a broader understanding of contemporary techniques on the part of the student, a realization that modern music is not arbitrary or whimsical in its structure. He will find, on the contrary, that it is as rational, systematic and easily grasped as any music studied in theory class. It is essential that students, the performers and creators of the future, be guided to this recognition; as Hindemith states, "something that cannot be understood by the analysis of a musician . . . cannot possibly be more convincing to the naïve listener."[5]

THE TEACHING OF MUSICAL ANALYSIS

The values of analytical study have so often been mentioned that there is no need to stress them here. Two prevalent misconceptions concerning analysis should be noted, however. The first of these is the belief that analysis, as a process of breaking down large phenomena into simpler components, destroys the music being dissected and consequently destroys the student's appreciation of the music. In answer to this contention it can first be pointed out that analysis is not music and that the analysis of a piece of music is not meant to substitute for the work itself. Abstracting the elements of a work is only the beginning of analysis. For, secondly, no analysis is complete until the components are reassembled and the abstraction again related to the concrete reality, i.e. the musical work, from which it derived. As Forte states,

What should be derived from analysis is simply increased understanding, which is, after all, what we derive from all adequate study tools . . . an effective analysis synthesizes: it provides new insights which, in a process of reorganization and consolidation, lead to greater knowledge.[6]

The second misconception is the belief that analysis is too technical a field to be of use to the average music student, that only theory majors will profit from it. This is unfortunately true if the subject is poorly taught. But the value of analysis need not be restricted to the technical level alone; it should influence one's total musical personality and be reflected in such varied musical activities as performing, composing, conducting, sight reading and critical listening. The fruits of analysis should be practically applied, in the same way that all acquired factual, verbal knowledge should result in changed behavior — new non-verbal habits, responses and attitudes.

If this is assumed, it then follows that analytical studies should be encouraged, that they should .be offered in college music curricula. Courses listed as "Form and Analysis" should deal with analysis as well as form; very often, however, such courses are exclusively concerned with a survey of musical forms. Analysis, if it is covered at all, may be no more than the analysis of form. Compared with the innumerable books that deal with form, there are relatively few textbooks or references devoted to techniques of analysis.

Analysis, as studied on the undergraduate level, must be concerned with all the factors — melodic, harmonic, textural, rhythmic and formal — that constitute the structure of an individual work or an individual composer's style. Historical and personal factors may be considered as well. The object of such study is the recognition of stylistic differences and individual practices, complementing the recognition of common practice which is developed in less advanced harmony and counterpoint courses. The common practice approach is useful and necessary in the earlier stages of learning, but lest it leave the student with the impression that Haydn and Mozart (or Schubert and Schumann, Ravel and Debussy, *et al.*) are stylistically identical, it must be counterbalanced by more detailed analytical studies. The unique characteristics of an individual work, or a composer's style, should be isolated and recognized as the most important factors of all.

The method of analysis used in this study can be easily employed in an undergraduate class in Form and Analysis. It is assumed that students in such a class have a general background in harmony and counterpoint, perhaps even an acquaintance with contemporary techniques. Concurrently with the usual survey of musical forms, class sessions would be spent in a discussion of the musical elements — melody, harmony, counterpoint, texture, rhythm, meter and tempo. In all cases, references would be made to individual practices: for example, J. S. Bach's approach to tonal counterpoint, as opposed to Handel's, a comparison of chromaticism in Mozart and Haydn, or the influence of Italian Bel Canto upon Chopin's melodic style.

At first, analyses of individual works by individual composers in terms of their form, stylistic features and structural details would be advisable. Eventually, students could attempt analysis of a selected body of music by a single composer, the main objective being a recognition of stylistic individuality. Composers of different historical periods and nationalities should be represented, and, for each individual composer, compositions in various media examined as well.

Analysis need not, of course, be restricted to courses in analysis, nor even occur within the framework of a course. Composers would benefit a great deal from analysis, even though they do not always admit it —

many of them, in fact, actively rejecting the notion. It would seem reasonable, however, that the study of composition involve reference to the ways of other composers, since a composition is always at least in part the product of experience — it is, in some degree, the expression not only of a unique idea but of one's reaction to other compositions.

If the student of composition wishes to extend and build upon his musical heritage, he must understand that heritage. Skill in analysis is an indispensable tool for complete understanding. Through analysis, the student will see that works establish their own terms, that composers express their unique selves even within the context of common practice, and that composers have themselves benefited from analysis of past practices.

THE TEACHING OF MUSIC LITERATURE AND APPRECIATION

It is now generally agreed that the music of our century is not esoteric, that it can be quite accessible to the larger listening public. This conviction has led to the inclusion of twentieth century trends and representative contemporary works in the curricula of listening courses — music appreciation, surveys of music history, and surveys of various areas of music literature, such as chamber music or the symphony. These courses are intended for the general undergraduate student body and seek to increase the students' understanding of musical styles and forms. In addition, the students' familiarity with the literature of music, including that of contemporary music, is broadened. The works of Ralph Vaughan Williams may be useful in illustrating basic problems that are discussed in such courses.

One such problem is that of the symphony or sonata in the twentieth century. Much contemporary music has been associated with the theater, ballet and opera, or is programmatic in nature. There is often a mistaken impression that the sonata, symphony and string quartet are, in our time, neglected media. And yet no survey of Sonata developments would be complete without reference to the achievements of Vaughan Williams, Sibelius, Prokofieff, Bartók and Hindemith.

Because the Vaughan Williams works clearly show their derivations from romantic tendencies, they would be valuable in such a survey. The development of the Sonata forms could be traced from the eighteenth century to the mid-twentieth century. It is obvious, in tracing this development, that the idea of the Sonata originally was directly related to tonality and tonal contrasts, although this initial impetus was somewhat obscured during the nineteenth century. Interestingly enough, the majority of contemporary works in the Sonata tradition are tonal in idiom, and the composers of these works write consistently tonal music. Moreover, these composers are interested in folk music, or, at the least, an expression of national characteristics in music.[7]

The writer is not advancing any judgments here; the following argument, however, is excellent for stimulating classroom discussion: that the Sonata forms, in all periods and styles, depend upon tonality for their justification; that a composer sensitive to folk music is more likely to retain tonality in his own music than other composers of our time; and that, therefore, the twentieth century nationalists have most successfully advanced and continued the Sonata tradition.

An equally sound argument could be advanced from the opposing viewpoint: that, in our time, conflict and contrast may be obtained through other than tonal means. Through the artful use of dynamics, instrumentation, rhythm and tempo, large-scale Sonata forms may be built in an atonal or polytonal style. In support of this thesis, the student and teacher may draw upon the works of Schönberg, Berg, Milhaud and Stravinsky, among others. It is, of course, essential that the student see *both* sides of the question.

There should be no doubt at this point that the teaching of the Vaughan Williams symphonies should stress content as well as techniques. While the concept of "programmism" in music must be restricted to its proper use, "meaning" in music must not be anathema. If music, as one of the humanities, offers the perceptive listener deeper insight into the history of ideas, one must admit that these ideas are manifested in quartets, concertos, sonatas and symphonies.[8] This is none the less true because many listeners draw different implications from the same work. True understanding, or appreciation, always results from the *interaction* of the character of the audience and the nature of the art work. This is as true of music as it is of painting, poetry or sculpture.

Such insight into the expressive characteristics of abstract music should not be limited to students of music literature. Students of analysis must examine stylistic features as they *function expressively*. They will discover that a composer develops a personal vocabulary of expressive symbols.[9] They will then approach their stylistic analyses with insight into technical and expressive function. Finally, they will see the limitations of interpreting the composing process as one of technique alone. Their study of the symphonies of Ralph Vaughan Williams will foster this awareness, for as we have seen, the presence of meaning in his work is indisputable.

APPENDIX II

Measure References

Six tables have been compiled for use by the reader. Each of the six refers to a specific area of musical style, namely:

1. Modality and other Melodic Devices
2. Harmonic Devices
3. Contrapuntal Devices
4. Ostinati and Ground Bass
5. Musical Forms
6. Instrumentation

In each of the six areas, specific movements and measures of individual symphonies have been referred to. These measures are indicated by a Roman numeral, representing the movement, followed by Arabic numerals which refer to specific measures. Thus III 40-50 refers to measures 40-50 of the third movement of the work in question.

The tables do not list all possible examples, but rather those which figure prominently in the symphonies, which can be used to illustrate general musical principles, and which lend themselves most readily to discussion and analysis.

211

TABLE 1
Modality and other Melodic Devices

	Modes	Prominent Use of Specific Intervals	Alternating Major-Minor Inflections
Sea Symphony	I 59-75 (Aeolian) IV 51-85 (Dorian)	II 60-66 (Pentatonic)	
London Symphony	II 59-69 (Aeolian)	I 112-138 (Pentatonic) III 40- (perfect fourth)	
Pastoral Symphony	III 47-65 (Mixolydian) IV 1-5 (Aeolian)	I 1-12 (Pentatonic) II 2-7 (Pentatonic)	
Fourth Symphony		IV 24-52 (minor second) II 61-70 (augmented fourth)	IV 266-308 (major-minor third) II 61-70 (major-minor third)
Fifth Symphony	III 1-12 (Dorian) III 12-28 (Aeolian)	I 3-12 (Pentatonic) IV 1-7 (Pentatonic)	II 347-357 (major-minor third)
Sixth Symphony	III 109-169 (Phrygian)	III 1-20 (augmented fourth)	I 82-96 (major-minor third) II 1-23 (major-minor second
Sinfonia Antartica		I 159-184 (perfect fourth-fifth) II 81-97 (augmented triad) III 56-65 (augmented fourth)	IV 1-21 (major-minor third)
Eighth Symphony	II 5-22 (Phrygian) II 82-127 (Dorian)	IV 1-28 (Pentatonic)	
Ninth Symphony	IV 53-60 (Phrygian)	II 1-71 (Pentatonic)	I 32-39 (major-minor third) III 42-79 (perfect augmented fourth) IV 60-63 (major-minor third)

TABLE 2
HARMONIC DEVICES

	Parallel Chord Movement	Alternating Major-Minor Triads	Modal Harmonization
Sea Symphony	IV 104-112	I 1-4 II 1-7 III 1-10	II 128-132 IV 51-85
London Symphony	I 38-62 II 1-16 III 373-384 IV 103-110	II 25-39	II 59-69 IV 16-31 IV 70-85
Pastoral Symphony	I 1-8 I 25-28 II 8-14 IV 128-144		III 47-64
Fourth Symphony	I 145-155 II 131-138 III 78-100 IV 177-188		II 61-69 IV 1-14
Fifth Symphony	II 169-172 IV 91-100	III 1-12	I 185-207 III 1-12 IV 91-105
Sixth Symphony	I 47-60 II 28-42 III 302-338 IV 49-57		I 160-188
Sinfonia Antartica	I 1-8 I 81-86 III 65-70	I 1-8 IV 1-37 V 28-42	
Eighth Symphony		I 22-35 I 134-140 III 1-13 III 32-35	I 108-132 I 252-284 II 1-65 IV 1-95
Ninth Symphony	I 124-133 II 8-10 II 54-60 III 268-277		I 10-15 IV 234-240

TABLE 3

CONTRAPUNTAL DEVICES

	Canonic Imitation	Stretto	Fugato	Rhythmic Augmentation & Diminution
Sea Symphony		I 21-33 I 320-330 II 85-99 IV 482-500	I 269-310 IV 135-147	
London Symphony		I 178-197 I 325-345 III 196-208		I 380-384 II 74-87 III 196-208
Pastoral Symphony	I 28-50 II 22-60 III 27-40 IV 14-55		III 173-212	
Fourth Symphony		I 67-83 II 27-45 III 92-100 IV 88-105	III 149-214 IV 309-464	IV 309-464
Fifth Symphony	I 12-21 I 135-147 II 1-25 III 32-38 IV 162-170	I 12-18 III 32-38 III 144-148		
Sixth Symphony	II 67-75 II 103-115 IV 45-65 IV 73-85		III 1-20 III 192-220 IV 1-39	
Sinfonia Antartica	IV 112-131	III 56-65 IV 13-21 IV 112-127 V 24-28		
Eighth Symphony	I 73-96 I 108-182 III 1-31		II 82-127 II 164-175	II 82-127 II 164-175
Ninth Symphony	I 40-45 II 67-80 IV 1-15 IV 53-63		I 1-10 III 126-143	

TABLE 4
Ostinati and Ground Bass

	Ground Bass	Rapid Figurations	Rhythmic or "Oom-Pah" Patterns
Sea Symphony		IV 403-444	
London Symphony			I 38-75
Pastoral Symphony	I 164-179	II 22-44	IV 118-130
Fourth Symphony	II 7-25	III 40-77	I 49-79 I 84-123 IV 20-45
Fifth Symphony	IV 1-67 (Passacaglia)	II 184-210 IV 153-168	
Sixth Symphony		I 1-42 III 109-169	I 43-160 II 86-130
Sinfonia Antartica		I 94-101 II 2-15 III 22-50	IV 82-92 V 52-88
Eighth Symphony		I 44-78 IV 29-42 IV 105-127 IV 176-192	II 1-18 II 34-73
Ninth Symphony		III 111-116	I 103-123 II 106-116 III 195-233 IV 26-34

TABLE 5
MUSICAL FORMS

	Sonata-Allegro	Sonatine	Part-Forms	Variations	Other
Sea Symphony	I (only Th. I in recapitulation)	III	II Ternary ABA form		IV in 2 large sections: 1. Sonata-Allegro 2. Arch-form
London Symphony	I (many motives)		II Ternary ABA form III Scherzo with 2 trios (ABACA) IV Ternary ABA form		Epilogue (Coda following movement IV)
Pastoral Symphony	I IV		II ABAB III Scherzo with repeated trio (ABABA)		
Fourth Symphony	I (Th. II much slower in recapitulation) II IV		III Scherzo and Trio (ABA)		Fugal Epilogue following movement IV
Fifth Symphony	III	I	II Scherzo with 2 trios (ABACA)	IV Passacaglia (variations in 3 large sections)	Epilogue (coda following movement IV)

TABLE 5, cont.

MUSICAL FORMS

	Sonata-Allegro	Sona-tine	Part-Forms	Varia-tions	Other
Sixth Symphony		I	II Ternary ABA III Scherzo with repeated Trio ABAB		IV Sectional ABCD
Sinfonia Antartica			II Scherzo and Trio ABA III Five part ABCBA IV Ternary ABA V March & Trio ABA		I Sectional ABC
Eighth Symphony		III	II Scherzo and Trio ABA IV Rondo ABACADA	I (may also be interpreted as Sonata-Allegro)	
Ninth Symphony	I		II Song with repeated Trio ABAB III Scherzo and Trio ABA		IV in 2 large sections 1. ABAB 2. Sonata-Allegro

TABLE 6

INSTRUMENTATION (solo passages)

	Solo Winds	Solo Brass	Solo Strings and Harp	Organ & Voice
Sea Symphony		II 54-59 (horn)	I 320-325 (viola)	I 67-221 (voice & chorus) III (entire chorus)
London Symphony	II 4-8 (English horn)		I 225-242 (Harp) II 145-151 (viola)	
Pastoral Symphony		II 67-77 (natural trumpet) II 112-122 (natural horn)		IV 3-5 (voice)
Fourth Symphony	II 61-69 (flute)	III 149-156 (tuba)		
Fifth Symphony	III 7-12 (English horn)	III 116-125 (horn & trumpet)	III 178-191 (violin)	
Sixth Symphony	IIl 109-170 (saxophone) IV 49-56 (oboe)		IV 40-49 (cello)	
Sinfonia Antartica	II 133-136 (bassoon) III 85-92 (flute)		IV 41-53 (violin)	III 127-142 (organ) I 69-85 (wordless chorus)
Eighth Symphony	II 5-21 (bassoon)	II 34-54 (trumpet)	III 62-83 (violin) III 106-109 (cello)	
Ninth Symphony	I 10-15 III 125-143 IV 234-241 (saxophone choir) I 32-40 (clarinet)	II 1-15 (flugelhorn)	I 134-147 (violin)	

NOTES

NOTES

Preface

1. See Hubert Foss, *Ralph Vaughan Williams — A Study* (London: Oxford University Press, 1950); Frank Howes, *The Music of Ralph Vaughan Williams* (London: Oxford University Press, 1954); James Day, *Vaughan Williams* (London: J. M. Dent & Sons, 1961); A. E. F. Dickinson, *Ralph Vaughan Williams* (London: Faber, Ltd., 1963).
2. Ernest Newman, *From the World of Music* (New York: Coward-McCann, Inc., 1957), pp. 15, 20.

PART ONE: THE HISTORICAL CONTEXT

The English Musical Tradition

Epigraph: Wilfrid Mellers, *Romanticism and the Twentieth Century* (Fairlawn, N.J.: Essential Books, 1957), p. 181.

1. Walker, *A History of Music in England* (London: Oxford University Press, 1924), p. 183.
2. Hugo Leichtentritt, *Music of the Western Nations* (Cambridge, Mass.: Harvard University Press, 1956), p. 183. See also Gustave Reese, *Music in the Renaissance* (New York: W. W. Norton, 1959 revised ed.), p. 763.
3. Eric Blom, *Music in England* (London: Penguin Books, Ltd., 1947 revised ed.), p. 33.
4. Leichtentritt, *op. cit.,* p. 184.
5. Blom, *op. cit.,* pp. 77-78.
6. *Ibid.,* p. 95.
7. Walker, *op. cit.,* p. 181.
8. See also Manfred Bukofzer, *Music in the Baroque Era* (New York: W. W. Norton, 1947), p. 187, in which a different theory is advanced. Bukofzer contends that English opera lacked "the spiritual center of a representative court. The restored English court was politically weak . . . in spite of its aping of French manners . . . it is symbolic that Purcell's *Dido and Aeneas* was not written for the court but for amateurs."

221

9. See Blom, *op. cit.,* p. 100, for a rough estimate of Purcell's output. Cf. Walker, *op. cit.,* pp. 138-39, for a more detailed listing.

10. J. A. Fuller Maitland, *English Music in the Nineteenth Century* (New York: E. P. Dutton & Co., 1902), p. 36.

11. Blom, *op. cit.,* p. 114.

12. Leichtentritt, *op. cit.,* p. 189.

13. It may be more accurate to place the blame not on Handel, but on the circumstances which made a Handel possible. See Donald F. Tovey, *Essays in Musical Analysis* (London: Oxford University Press, 1935), II, 8. "We hear a great deal about the way in which English music was 'crushed by the ponderous genius of Handel.' It was crushed by nothing of the sort; it was crushed simply by the fact that the rank and fashion of English music patrons would for centuries listen only to Italian singers and Italian composers. Handel's methods were Italian, and he benefited accordingly."

14. Wilfrid Mellers, *Music and Society: England and the European Tradition* (London: Dennis Dobson, Ltd., 1946), p. 97.

15. *Ibid.,* p. 158 (note 36).

16. Cecil Sharp, *English Folk Songs* (London: Novello and Co., 1920).

The Education of Vaughan Williams

1. Ralph Vaughan Williams, "Musical Autobiography," in Foss, *Ralph Vaughan Williams,* p. 22. The autobiographical sketch appears as Chapter 3 of Foss's book, pp. 18-38. Further references to that autobiography will not be documented.

2. Foss, *op. cit.,* p. 14.

3. Or, in Foss's words (*op. cit.,* pp. 71-72): "Two distinct strands can be discerned in these hymnological labours — the influence of Bach and the influence of folk music. Bach's idiom, we know, came to him as something instantly recognizable. . . . On the other hand, the natural gaiety, spontaneity, and modernity of feeling in the carol could attract him no less."

4. For a study of Holst's place in the development of English music in this century and of his relation to Vaughan Williams, see Mellers, *Romanticism and the Twentieth Century,* pp. 174-81. See also Norman Demuth, *Musical Trends in the Twentieth Century* (London: Rockliff Publishing Corp., Ltd., 1952), pp. 136-54.

5. A. E. F. Dickinson, *An Introduction to the Music of Ralph Vaughan Williams,* Musical Pilgrim Series (London: Oxford University Press, 1928), p. 6.

PART TWO: THE NINE SYMPHONIES

A Sea Symphony

1. William Kimmel, "Vaughan Williams' Choice of Words," *Music & Letters,* XIX (April, 1938), 139-41.
2. Compare the Vaughan Williams texts and the Whitman poems from which they are drawn: "Song of the Exposition," "A Song for All Seas, All Ships," "On the Beach at Night Alone," "After the Sea-ship" (all from *Sea Drift*), and "The Explorers" (from *Passage to India*).
3. Dickinson, *An Introduction to the Music of Ralph Vaughan Williams,* p. 6.
4. *Ibid.,* p. 10.
5. This use of the whole-tone scale in Vaughan Williams' earlier music, like the use of parallel chord progressions, may be traced to his period of study with Ravel. See Edmund Rubbra, "The Later Vaughan Williams," *Music & Letters,* XVIII (January 1937), 3, and cf. Robinson Hawthorne, "A Note on the Music of Vaughan Williams," *The Music Review,* IX (November, 1948), 269.
6. This term refers to a ternary musical form in which the final section presents the themes or elements of the first section, but in the inverse order of their initial appearance.
7. Howes, *The Music of Ralph Vaughan Williams* (p. 3), suggests that the movement could be performed independently as a separate cantata.
8. It may well have been passages such as this that caused Parry to write of the symphony in 1914: "Big stuff, but full of impertinences as well as noble moments." See Foss, *Ralph Vaughan Williams,* p. 93.
9. At this point, the optional cut in the score (beginning at measure 337) ends.
10. *Musical America,* XIII (December 3, 1910), 31.
11. Percy M. Young, *Vaughan Williams* (London: Dennis Dobson, Ltd., 1953), pp. 53-54.
12. D. Hugh Ottaway, "Vaughan Williams' Symphonies," *Disc,* V (1952), 150.

A London Symphony

1. Foss, *Ralph Vaughan Williams,* p. 109.

2. Howes, *The Music of Ralph Vaughan Williams,* p. 21.
3. *Ibid.,* p. 17.
4. Foss, *op. cit.,* p. 132.
5. Howes (*op. cit.,* p. 18) recalls that Elgar similarly referred to street music in the *Cockaigne Overture,* and finds it sociologically interesting that Cockney music is regarded as essential to a musical portrayal of Edwardian London.
6. A comparison of the present suggestion of Big Ben with the one heard in the opening movement will reveal that the chimes are now sounding a later quarter-hour, which may suggest that the symphony portrays the passage of time in the life of the city.
7. Foss, *op. cit.,* p. 133.
8. Ottaway. "Vaughan Williams' Symphonies," p. 150.
9. As recorded in Percy A. Scholes, *New Works by Modern British Composers,* Series I (London: Stainer & Bell, 1921), p. 23.
10. Foss, *op. cit.,* p. 32.
11. Howes, *op. cit.,* p. 11.
12. W. R. Anderson, "Vaughan Williams' London Symphony," *Hallé,* October, 1946, p. 17.

Pastoral Symphony

1. Foss, *Ralph Vaughan Williams,* p .135.
2. *Ibid.,* p. 134.
3. Howes, *The Music of Ralph Vaughan Williams,* p. 23.
4. Tovey, *Essays in Musical Analysis,* II, 130.
5. In concert pitch, of course, these would be D-flat (7th partial) and F (9th partial).
6. Howes, *op. cit.,* p. 23.
7. It is suggested in the score that the passage may also be "played by 1st Clarinet, when there is no vocal Soloist."
8. Neville Cardus, "The Measure of Vaughan Williams," *The Saturday Review,* July 31, 1954, p. 46.
9. D. Hugh Ottaway. "Vaughan Williams' Pastoral Symphony," *Hallé,* December, 1951, p. 4.
10. Herbert Howells, "Vaughan Williams' Pastoral Symphony," *Music & Letters,* III (April, 1922), 123.
11. D. Hugh Ottaway, "Vaughan Williams and the Pastoral Symphony," *The Musical Times,* XC (November, 1949), 404. On this same subject, Mellers, *Romanticism,* p. 176, has noted that "even though one may recognize groups of themes which can be equated with the conventional first and second subjects, there is no hint of sonata conflict."

12. Foss, *op. cit.,* pp. 65-96.
13. *Ibid.,* pp. 133-34.

Symphony in F Minor, Number 4

1. Vaughan Williams did not number most of the symphonies, but designated them either by key or title. Numbers have been added parenthetically to untitled symphonies, and such works will be referred to here by number as well as by key.
2. Howes, *The Music of Ralph Vaughan Williams,* p. 29.
3. *Ibid.,* p. 1.
4. Foss, *Ralph Vaughan Williams,* pp. 124, 138.
5. Mellers, *Romanticism,* p. 177.
6. Foss, *op. cit.,* pp. 137-38.
7. D. Hugh Ottaway, "Vaughan Williams' Symphony in F Minor," *Hallé,* November, 1950, p. 13.
8. N. Gerrard Long, "Vaughan Williams' Fourth Symphony — A Study in Interpretation," *The Monthly Musical Record,* LXXVII (June, 1947), 120-21.
9. Howes (*op. cit.,* p. 33) suggests that motive A is "horizontal" in its contour and motive B "vertical," concluding that the symphony, like a work of architecture, is "braced in both directions."
10. Ralph Vaughan Williams and Gustav Holst, *Heirs and Rebels,* ed. Ursula Vaughan Williams and Imogen Holst (London: Oxford University Press, 1959), p. 84.
11. David Ewen, *The Complete Book of 20th Century Music* (Englewood Cliffs, N.J.: Prentice-Hall, Inc., 1960), p. 450.

Symphony in D Major, Number 5

1. Foss, *Ralph Vaughan Williams,* p. 144.
2. The term is used here to refer to a Sonata-Allegro without a development, but with a lengthy transition in its place.
3. See Part III of this volume, Harmony.
4. Howes, *The Music of Ralph Vaughan Williams,* p. 46.
5. *Ibid.,* p. 51.
6. The apparently contradictory statement that the seven-measure ground melody is stated ten times in 68 bars requires further explanation: not all of the variations are seven measures in length, especially after the first four variations.
7. Demuth, *Musical Trends,* p. 151.
8. Foss, *op. cit.,* p. 150.

9. Howes, *op. cit.,* pp. 42-43.
10. Cardus, *The Measure of Vaughan Williams,* p. 48.
11. D. Hugh Ottaway, "Vaughan Williams' Symphony in D and 'The Pilgrim's Progress,'" *The Musical Times,* XCIV (October, 1953), 456.
12. Young, *Vaughan Williams,* p. 162.
13. Ralph Vaughan Williams, *Some Thoughts on Beethoven's Choral Symphony, and Other Writings* (London: Oxford University Press, 1953), p. 7.

Symphony in E Minor, Number 6

1. Howes, *The Music of Ralph Vaughan Williams,* p. 53.
2. Herbert Howells, "Vaughan Williams," *The Score,* No. 7, December, 1952, p. 57.
3. Demuth, *Musical Trends,* p. 148.
4. Foss, *Ralph Vaughan Williams,* p. 150.
5. Howes, *op. cit.,* p. 55.
6. Deryck Cooke, *The Language of Music* (London: Oxford University Press, 1959), p. 267.
7. A. E. F. Dickinson, "Toward the Unknown Region, An Introduction to Vaughan Williams' Sixth Symphony," *The Music Review,* IX (November, 1948), 289.
8. Scott Goddard, "Vaughan Williams' Sixth Symphony," *Hallé,* May, 1948, p. 5.
9. Howes, *op. cit.,* p. 62.
10. *Ibid.,* pp. 64-66, 364.

Sinfonia Antartica, Number 7

1. Howes, *The Music of Ralph Vaughan Williams,* p. 68.
2. Another resemblance between the two Scherzo movements may be found in a similar use of the whole-tone scale, particularly in rapid figurations.
3. Howes, *op. cit.,* p. 74,
4. Cooke, *The Language of Music,* p. 266. See also Howes, *op. cit.,* p. 67.
5. Cooke, *op. cit.,* p. 261.
6. In the film score, this motive represented a death knell for a member of the expedition named Captain Oates. See Howes, *op. cit.,* p. 78.
7. This motive, in the film, accompanied the blizzard that eventually overcame and defeated the expedition. See James Day, *Vaughan Williams,* p. 149.

8. Howes, *op. cit.*, p. 67. See also Day, *op. cit.*, pp. 147-50.
9. Colin Mason, "Vaughan Williams' 'Sinfonia Antartica,'" *The Musical Times,* XCIV (March, 1953), 128.
10. Michael Kennedy, "Vaughan Williams at Eighty-Five," *The Musical Times,* XCVIII (October, 1957), 546.

Symphony in D Minor, Number 8

1. A. E. F. Dickinson, "Ralph Vaughan Williams," *The Musical Quarterly,* XLV (January, 1959), 2.
2. D. Hugh Ottaway, "Vaughan Williams' Eighth Symphony," *Music & Letters,* XXXVIII (July, 1957), 213.
3. Day, *Vaughan Williams,* p. 162.
4. Kennedy, "Vaughan Williams at Eighty-Five," p. 545.

Symphony in E Minor, Number 9

1. Dickinson, "Ralph Vaughan Williams," p. 6.
2. Day, *Vaughan Williams,* p. 166.

PART THREE: STRUCTURE, STYLE AND MEANING

Structural Considerations

1. Geoffrey Crankshaw, "Vaughan Williams and His Symphonies," *Musical Opinion,* LXXV (July, 1952), 31. Cf. Howes, *The Music of Ralph Vaughan Williams,* pp. 54-55.
2. There are two slow movements in the Sixth Symphony; the second movement is the ABA referred to here. The slow Epilogue is sectional in form, as previously noted.
3. The *text* of the Finale also illuminates, explains and unifies the three preceding poems. See Part II of this volume, *A Sea Symphony.*
4. Foss, *Ralph Vaughan Williams,* p. 43.
5. For example, the conspicuous semitone motive in the Fifth Symphony, an otherwise consistently diatonic work, has been associated with Bunyan's "foul fiends" and "hobgoblins." See Part II, Symphony Number 5 in D major.
6. The technique consistently appears in music of the Tudor school; it is a common feature in Purcell. See A. E. F. Dickinson, "The Vaughan Williams Tradition," *Monthly Musical Record,* LXIX (September and October, 1939), 205-206, 237-39.

7. Demuth, *Musical Trends,* pp. 146-47. See also William J. Edmonds, "Harmony in the Symphonies of Ralph Vaughan Williams," (Master's thesis, North Texas State College, 1958), pp. 43-45.
8. Rubert O. Erlebach, "Vaughan Williams and His Three Symphonies," *Monthly Musical Record,* LII (June, 1922), 127.
9. Young, *Vaughan Williams,* p. 160.
10. Elsie Payne, "Vaughan Williams' Orchestral Colourings," *Monthly Musical Record,* LXXXIV (January, 1954), 3.
11. Young, *op. cit.,* p. 179.
12. *Ibid.,* p. 180.
13. *Ibid.,* p. 156.
14. Howes, *The Music of Ralph Vaughan Williams,* pp. 43, 60.
15. Edmonds, *op. cit.,* p. 65.

Sources and Evolution of the Style

1. Foss, *Ralph Vaughan Williams,* p. 44.
2. *Ibid.,* p. 67.
3. Vaughan Williams, *Some Thoughts on Beethoven's Choral Symphony,* p. 131.
4. Dickinson, "The Vaughan Williams Tradition," pp. 237-38.
5. Vaughan Williams and Holst, *Heirs and Rebels,* p. 83.
6. D. Hugh Ottaway, "Vaughan Williams and the European Background," *Hallé,* July, 1951, p. 13.
7. Demuth, *Musical Trends,* pp. 144-46.
8. Cf. Howes, *The Music of Ralph Vaughan Williams,* p. 1 and Foss, *op. cit.,* p. 122.
9. Foss, *op. cit.,* p. 122.
10. Payne, "Vaughan Williams' Orchestral Colourings," pp. 3-5. See also Foss., *op. cit.,* pp. 29, 37-38.

The Problem of Meaning

1. Ernest Newman, *More Essays from the World of Music* (New York: Coward-McCann, Inc., 1958), pp. 125-26.
2. Neville Cardus, *Talking of Music* (London: Collins Publishers, Ltd., 1959), p. 213.
3. H. C. Colles, *The Oxford History of Music* (London: Oxford University Press, 1934), VII, 165.
4. Dickinson, "Toward the Unknown Region," pp. 281-82.
5. Howells, "Vaughan Williams," p. 57.

6. Hubert Foss, "Vaughan Williams and the Orchestra," *Penguin Magazine,* IX (July, 1949), 31.
7. Howes, *The Music of Ralph Vaughan Williams,* pp. 1-3.
8. Ralph Vaughan Williams, *National Music* (London: Oxford University Press, 1959), pp. 23-36.

APPENDIX I

Educational Implications

1. See Howard A. Murphy and Edwin J. Stringham, *Creative Harmony and Musicianship* (Englewood Cliffs, N.J.: Prentice-Hall, 1958), Chapter XX, pp. 338-60.
2. See Leon Dallin, *Techniques of Twentieth Century Composition* (Dubuque, Iowa: Wm. C. Brown Co., 1957), pp. 88-108, and cf. Vincent Persichetti, *Twentieth Century Harmony* (New York: W. W. Norton, 1961), pp. 182-212.
3. John Vincent, *The Diatonic Modes in Modern Music* (New York: Mills Music, Inc., 1951), pp. 16-56. Cf. Dallin, *op. cit.,* pp. 20-33, 96-100.
4. Persichetti, *op. cit.,* pp. 66-81.
5. Paul Hindemith, *Craft of Musical Composition* (New York: Associated Music Publishers, 1945), I, 2.
6. Allen Forte, *Contemporary Tone Structures* (New York: Teachers College Bureau of Publications, 1955), p. 1.
7. Cf. Gerald Abraham, ed., *The Music of Sibelius* (New York: W. W. Norton, 1947); Israel Nestyev, *Sergei Prokofiev* (New York: Alfred A. Knopf, Inc., 1946); Halsey Stevens, *The Life and Music of Béla Bartók* (New York: Oxford University Press, 1953).
8. See Donald N. Ferguson, *Music as Metaphor* (Minneapolis: University of Minnesota Press, 1960); cf. Leonard B. Meyer, *Emotion and Meaning in Music* (Chicago: University of Chicago Press, 1956).
9. See Deryck Cooke, *The Language of Music,* for a detailed approach to content analysis.

A SELECTED
BIBLIOGRAPHY

A SELECTED BIBLIOGRAPHY

ABRAHAM, GERALD (ed.). *The Music of Sibelius.* New York: W. W. Norton, 1947.

ANDERSON, W. R. "Vaughan Williams' London Symphony," *Hallé,* October, 1946.

BLOM, ERIC. *Music in England.* London: Penguin Books, Ltd., 1947.

BUKOFZER, MANFRED. *Music in the Baroque Era.* New York: W. W. Norton & Co., 1947.

CARDUS, NEVILLE. "The Measure of Vaughan Williams," *The Saturday Review,* July 31, 1954.

————. *Talking of Music.* London: Collins Publishers, Ltd., 1959.

COLLES, H. C. *The Oxford History of Music,* VII. London: Oxford University Press, 1934.

COOKE, DERYCK. *The Language of Music.* London: Oxford University Press, 1959.

CRANKSHAW, GEOFFREY. "Vaughan Williams and His Symphonies," *Musical Opinion,* LXXV, July, 1952.

DALLIN, LEON. *Techniques of Twentieth Century Composition.* Dubuque, Iowa: Wm. C. Brown Co., 1957.

DAY, JAMES. *Vaughan Williams.* London: J. M. Dent & Sons, 1961.

DEMUTH, NORMAN. *Musical Trends in the Twentieth Century.* London: Rockliff Publishing Corp., Ltd., 1952.

DICKINSON, A. E. F. *An Introduction to the Music of Ralph Vaughan Williams.* Musical Pilgrim Series. London: Oxford University Press, 1928.

————. *Ralph Vaughan Williams.* London: Faber, Ltd., 1963.

————. "Ralph Vaughan Williams," *The Musical Quarterly,* XLV, January, 1959.

————. "Toward the Unknown Region, An Introduction to Vaughan Williams' Sixth Symphony," *The Music Review,* IX, November, 1948.

————. "Vaughan Williams' Fifth Symphony," *The Music Review,* VI, February, 1945.

———. "The Vaughan Williams Tradition," *Monthly Musical Record*, LXIX, September and October, 1939.

EDMONDS, WILLIAM J. "Harmony in the Symphonies of Ralph Vaughan Williams," Unpublished Master's thesis, North Texas State College, 1958.

ERLEBACH, RUPERT O. "Vaughan Williams and His Three Symphonies," *Monthly Musical Record*, LII, June, 1922.

EWEN, DAVID. *The Complete Book of 20th Century Music,* Englewood Cliffs, N.J.: Prentice-Hall, Inc., 1960.

FERGUSON, DONALD N. *Music as Metaphor.* Minneapolis: University of Minnesota Press, 1962.

FORTE, ALLEN. *Contemporary Tone Structures.* New York: Teachers College Bureau of Publications, 1955.

FOSS, HUBERT. *Ralph Vaughan Williams — A Study.* London: Oxford University Press, 1950.

———. "Vaughan Williams and the Orchestra," *Penguin Magazine,* No. 9, July, 1949.

———. "Vaughan Williams' D Major Symphony," *Hallé,* August, 1950.

FULLER-MAITLAND, J. A. *English Music in the Nineteenth Century.* New York: E. P. Dutton & Co., 1902.

GODDARD, SCOTT. "Vaughan Williams' Sixth Symphony," *Hallé,* May, 1948.

HAWTHORNE, ROBINSON. "A Note on the Music of Vaughan Williams," *The Music Review,* IX, November, 1948.

HILL, RALPH (ed.). *The Symphony.* London: Penguin Books, Ltd., 1950.

HINDEMITH, PAUL. *Craft of Musical Composition,* Vol. I. New York: Associated Music Publishers, 1945.

HOWELLS, HERBERT. "Vaughan Williams," *The Score,* No. 7, December, 1952.

———. "Vaughan Williams' Pastoral Symphony," *Music & Letters,* III, April, 1922.

HOWES, FRANK. *The Music of Ralph Vaughan Williams.* London: Oxford University Press, 1954.

KENNEDY, MICHAEL. "Vaughan Williams at Eighty-Five," *The Musical Times,* XCVIII, October, 1957.

KIMMEL, WILLIAM. "Vaughan Williams' Choice of Words," *Music & Letters,* XIX, April, 1938.

LANG, PAUL HENRY. *Music in Western Civilization.* New York: W. W. Norton & Co., 1941.

LEICHTENTRITT, HUGO. *Music, History and Ideas.* Cambridge, Mass.: Harvard University Press, 1958.

———. *Music of the Western Nations.* Cambridge, Mass.: Harvard University Press, 1956.

LONG, N. GERRARD. "Vaughan Williams' Fourth Symphony — A Study in Interpretation," *The Monthly Musical Record,* LXXVII, June, 1947.

MASON, COLIN. "Vaughan Williams' 'Sinfonia Antartica,'" *The Musical Times,* XCIV, March, 1953.

MELLERS, WILFRID. *Music and Society: England and the European Tradition.* London: Dennis Dobson, Ltd., 1946.

———. *Romanticism and the Twentieth Century.* Fairlawn, N.J.: Essential Books, 1957.

MEYER, LEONARD B. *Emotion and Meaning in Music.* Chicago: University of Chicago Press, 1956.

MURPHY, HOWARD A. and STRINGHAM, EDWIN J. *Creative Harmony and Musicianship.* Englewood Cliffs, N.J.: Prentice-Hall, 1958.

Musical America, XIII, December 3, 1910.

NESTYEV, ISRAEL. *Sergei Prokofiev.* New York: Alfred A. Knopf, Inc., 1946.

NEWMAN, ERNEST. *From the World of Music.* New York: Coward-McCann, Inc., 1957.

———. *More Essays from the World of Music.* New York: Coward-McCann, Inc., 1958.

OTTAWAY, D. HUGH. "Vaughan Williams' Eighth Symphony," *Music & Letters,* XXXVIII, July, 1957.

———. "Vaughan Williams and the European Background," *Hallé,* July, 1951.

———. "Vaughan Williams and the Pastoral Symphony," *The Musical Times,* XC, November, 1949.

———. "Vaughan Williams' Pastoral Symphony," *Hallé,* December, 1951.

———. "Vaughan Williams Symphony in D and 'The Pilgrim's Progress,'" *The Musical Times,* XCIV, October, 1953.

————. "Vaughan Williams' Symphony in F Minor," *Hallé*, November, 1950.

————. "Vaughan Williams' Symphonies," *Disc*, V, Nos. 20, 21, 22, 1952-3.

PAYNE, ELSIE. "Vaughan Williams and Folk Song," *The Music Review*, XV, May, 1954.

————. "Vaughan Williams' Orchestral Colourings," *Monthly Musical Record*, LXXXIV, January, 1954.

PERSICHETTI, VINCENT. *Twentieth Century Harmony.* New York: W. W. Norton & Co., 1961.

REESE, GUSTAVE. *Music in the Renaissance.* New York: W. W. Norton & Co., 1959.

RUBBRA, EDMUND. "The Later Vaughan Williams," *Music & Letters*, XVIII, January, 1937.

SCHOLES, PERCY A. *New Works by Modern British Composers*, Series I. London: Stainer & Bell, 1921.

SHARP, CECIL. *English Folk Songs.* London: Novello and Co., 1920.

SMITH, LORRAINE. "Vaughan Williams, An English Composer," Masters Essay, Columbia University, 1933.

STEVENS, HALSEY. *The Life and Music of Béla Bartók.* New York: Oxford University Press, 1953.

STRANGWAYS, A. H. FOX. "English Folksongs," *Music & Letters*, V, October, 1924.

TOVEY, DONALD F. *Essays in Musical Analysis*, Vols. I and II. London: Oxford University Press, 1935.

VAUGHAN WILLIAMS, RALPH. *The Making of Music.* Ithaca, New York: Cornell University Press, 1955.

————. *National Music.* London: Oxford University Press, 1959.

————. *Some Thoughts on Beethoven's Choral Symphony, and Other Writings.* London: Oxford University Press, 1953.

VAUGHAN WILLIAMS, RALPH, and HOLST, GUSTAVE. *Heirs and Rebels*, ed. Ursula Vaughan Williams and Imogen Holst. London: Oxford University Press, 1959.

VINCENT, JOHN. *The Diatonic Modes in Modern Music.* New York: Mills Music, Inc., 1951.

WALKER, ERNEST. *A History of Music in England.* London: Oxford University Press, 1924.

YOUNG, PERCY M. *Vaughan Williams.* London: Dennis Dobson, Ltd., 1953.

INDEX

INDEX

Abraham, Gerald, 229
Aeolian mode, 23, 26, 51, 54, 91, 98, 100, 139, 206
Analysis: method used, purposes, viii ff.; procedure of, 16; 205, 206; teaching of, 207 ff.
Anderson, W. R., 57
Anne, Queen (of England), 7
Ars antiqua, 4
Augmentation, Rhythmic, 44-45, 51-53, 61-62, 77-78, 86-87, 95, 97, 110, 115-116, 118-119, 143, 148, 159, 163

Bach, Johann Sebastian, 8, 11-12, 13, 105, 186-187, 208, 222
Bartók, Béla, 209
Bayreuth, 12
Beethoven, Ludwig van, 12, 57, 73, 104-105, 135, 167, 169-170, 188-190, 194, 196
Beggar's Opera, The, 7-8
Bel Canto, 208
Bennett, Sir William Sterndale, 9
Berg, Alban, 210
Berlin, 12
Berlioz, Hector, 9, 189
Binchois (Gilles de Binche), 4
Birmingham, 9
Blom, Eric 4, 5, 7
Bold Princess Royal, The, 30
Brahms, Johannes, 3, 170, 186, 189-190
Britten, Benjamin, 199

Bruch, Max, 12, 14, 173, 186
Bruckner, Anton, 3, 186, 189
Bukofzer, Manfred, 221
Bull, John, 5
Bunyan, John, 89, 94, 135, 196, 227
Butterworth, George, 39
Byrd, William, 4-5

Cadenza, unmeasured, 64, 69, 71, 80, 173, 180
Cambridge, 12
Canonic imitation, 35, 44, 51, 67-68, 71, 75-79, 83-85, 87, 94, 96, 98-100, 102, 114-116, 132, 152, 158, 160-162, 192. *See* Stretto imitation; Overlapping imitation
Cardus, Neville, 71, 104, 194
Charles I, 5-6
Charles II, 5-6, 7
Chopin, Frederic, 9, 208
Church of England, 5
Churchill, Sir Winston, 89
Colles, H. C., 194
Concerto for Tuba and Orchestra, 191
Cooke, Deryck, x, 117, 127-128, 229
Cowen, Sir Frederic, 10
Crankshaw, Geoffrey, 227
Cromwell, Oliver, 5-6
Cyclic motives: in specific works, 21, 40, 75; 164; tonalities related to, 185